LETS
GO
PUBLISH

The Bill of Rights By Founder James Madison

Refresh your knowledge of the specific rights granted to all Americans.

Read <u>the Bill of Rights by Founder James Madison</u> *so you understand your rights & your freedoms…so that no nerd in government can take them from you! This book is unabridged & annotated.*

Americans who hate corruption should love what the founders gave us in The Bill of Rights. Learn about your rights and freedoms by reading The Bill of Rights.

After understanding the Constitution, this is the best thing you can do to understand your role in assuring our great form of government. Our nation, our freedom and our liberties are being attacked today by corrupt left-leaning anti-American politicians. This book is one of the tools needed to stop them.

It does not get any better than reading this crisp copy of The Bill of Rights by James Madison. It is the best means for anybody who is reengaging with America or to give to a friend or relative who needs a nudge to understand what would be lost without our Constitution and Bill of Rights… or worst yet, without America as founded.

Even if you learned civics years ago, knowledge of which, by the way, is hard to find today, more than likely you are unsure of what America offers in the way of rights, and powers, and the duties for Americans to achieve them. This book has been written as a first step to help you be better prepared to react to the over-reach of corrupt politicians at the highest levels of government. Know your rights or lose your rights!

Without the knowledge that you can gain easily in this book, for example, you might think that your representatives in Congress hold all the cards, and that mum is the word. You may think that you can speak freely only in the free speech zones of American universities. If you feel pressure to behave in a politically-correct fashion, this book is your first antidote to coming out of the funk and the group-think, and thinking again for yourself.

Just because powerful elite officials, who are part of the corrupt establishment in both political Parties choose to ignore our rights and freedoms does not mean we must endure tyranny. The first step of course is to understand the most basic written precepts in the Constitution and the fully described Bill of Ten written by Patriot President James Madison well before he ascended to the presidency of the USA. Madison would tell you that today ladies & gentlemen, reading this book is a must.

LETS GO PUBLISH

BRIAN W. KELLY

Title: The Bill of Rights by Founder James Madison
Copyright © 2017   Brian W. Kelly
Publisher: Brian P. Kelly
Author   Brian W. Kelly

Published by: .... LETS GO PUBLISH!
Editor .... Brian P. Kelly
Email: .... info@letsgopublish.com
Web site .... www.letsgopublish.com
Cover Designer .... Brian W. Kelly

Library of Congress Copyright Information Pending

ISBN Information: The International Standard Book Number (ISBN) is a unique machine-readable identification number, which marks any book unmistakably. The ISBN is the clear standard in the book industry. 159 countries and territories are officially ISBN members. The Official ISBN for this book is on the outside cover:

ISBN: **978-1-947402-12-6**

The price for this work is:									**$8.95 USD**
10	9	8	7	6	5	4	3	2	1

Release Date: October 2017

Dedication

To the entire Kelly Family.
(My father's side of the family)

They have all stood there with me and I with them, as we seek the truth and continue our fight for our freedoms.

The gentlemen Kelly's on this list fought in World War II or the Korean War. We thank them deeply for their service.

Uncle Mart, Uncle Ed, Aunt Marie, Aunt Catherine, Aunt Helen, Uncle Pat, Uncle Mike, Uncle Phil, Uncle Joe, and Uncle Johnnie

God bless them all!

Acknowledgments

In every book that I write or edit, I publicly acknowledged all of the help that I have received from many sources. Some of these wonderful people are still on earth and others have made their way to heaven.

I would like to thank many people for helping me in this effort. I appreciate all the help that I received in putting this book together, along with the 126 other books from the past.

My printed acknowledgments were once so large that book readers needed to navigate too many pages to get to page one of the text. To permit me more flexibility, I put my acknowledgment list online at www.letsgopublish.com. The list of acknowledgments continues to grow. Believe it or not, it once cost about a dollar more to print each book.

Thank you all on the big list in the sky and God bless you all for your help.

Please check out www.letsgopublish.com to read the latest version of my heartfelt acknowledgments updated for this book. Thank you all!

In this book, I received some extra special help from many avid America supporters including Bruce Ikeda, Dennis Grimes, Gerry Rodski, Wily Ky Eyely, Angel Irene McKeown Kelly, Angel Edward Joseph Kelly Sr., Angel Edward Joseph Kelly Jr., Ann Flannery, Angel James Flannery Sr., Mary Daniels, Bill Daniels, Robert Gary Daniels, Angel Sarah Janice Daniels, Angel Punkie Daniels, Joe Kelly, Diane Kelly, Brian P. Kelly, Mike P. Kelly, Katie P. Kelly, Angel Ben Kelly, and Budmund (Buddy) Arthur Kelly.

Preface

We need to know our rights if for no other reason than to deny our politicians the opportunity to take them from us. Sometimes our current corrupt officials forget, that there are more of us than them so please do not get hoodwinked believing any of their spiel. They have no power but for what the people grant them. And we can un-elect on a regular basis and they are finished.

Once we the people are back in the game of life, knowing our rights, nobody will be able to take them away.

In a world where out of nowhere, one day white people began to be labeled as supremacists and a curse of a having experienced a white birth now causes a disease called white privilege, one wonders what went wrong. Having been brought up accidentally white, to believe that all men are created equal, I have no room for white supremacists nor black supremacists but it seems too many do. And a lot of that can be blamed on a wicked press and our poor leadership.

There are actually those who ask, "Why should Americans have lives that are nice when the rest of the world is suffering? Ask yourself, what part of your personal America are you willing to give up for nameless, faceless, people who could care a hoot about whether you live or die.

That's what it is all about today, folks. I hope that is why you are reading this book, written to counteract the influences of corrupt dirty politicians using rights written by one of our greatest founders, James Madison.

Why are the US press and the bulk of government workers so anti-American? Can you figure that one out? Black, Yellow, or White, maybe they should take up residence someplace else and torment another group of people.

Early Americans fought for our rights and later Americans fought to preserve them. Communists were never interested in protecting our rights in the beginning, the middle, and surely not now when many non-thinking Americans are prepared to hand our country over to the corrupt people in our government who represent them.

So, what rhetoric would you expect from those that espouse an ideology that says government should take from you so that Joe Dokes down the street should never have to worry about working? Joe Dokes will never have any rights other than the short term right to not work for his meager welfare payments.

Since neither Communism nor communism has ever worked in any country, you and I know that life won't always be sweet for Joe Dokes and Mary Dokes. However, neither Joe nor Mary know it and they would not believe you if you read the history of the world to them 100 or more times.

American rights are not a gift. They were not donated to Americans by anybody. Many Americans fought and many died for independence from the tyranny of England as well as in World Wars and other wars. America was always on the side of right and our great country still is on the side of right.

Once our own independence, freedoms, and liberties were gained from the bloodshed, the objective always was to keep the rest of the world safe and permit the whole world to live as well as it could in safety. America is a good country. America and Americans have helped our neighbors across the world from our moment our country was founded.

The graves of our sons and fathers and grandfathers with tombstones stretched across the world are vivid proof of our kindness as a country and our desire to help all the people of the world to become or to remain free. Don't let the *Blame America First* crowd talk down America while you are in the room. America and Americans deserve better.

Americans should not have to apologize to anybody. We should have no guilt. Yet, our bought and paid for corrupt press and our current corrupt government would love to ram tyranny down our throats by telling us we are bad people. Please don't buy any of it. We are not bad people.

We are exceptional people. Nobody has ever done in the existence of recorded history as much as America and Americans have done for our fellow man in America and across the world.

If you choose to wait until a Democrat, a progressive, a Marxist, or a communist says something good about America, you will be waiting a lifetime. Think about that while you consider if big government is really good for the people. Think again, please. Big government is good for big shots, big money, big corporations, big unions, a big corrupt press, and other big thinkers who hate America.

It has been 240 plus years since the United States, our country, achieved its independence. Along with independence, we the people, through the grace of our founders, earned freedom and liberty. Nobody has a right to demean US for that and nobody can take it away.

Ironically, there are some in America who espouse the liberal progressive Marxist ideology despite its demands that they give up on America. They are fully ready to blame America first for everything. They hate you and I and I bet you they do not even know why! They probably do not like anybody including themselves and their "best friends."

Ironically, here we are, 240 plus years after the Constitution and we still cannot get these people to agree that freedom is a good thing. Yet without freedom, they could not operate their clandestine socialist works in our country. As far as I am concerned it is OK if they all left town and went on to their favorite suppressed country to practice their ideology. They hurt America every day.

Though all is not perfect in America, the principles of the Constitution and the Bill of Rights are so sound and so powerful that even a knave politician cannot bring us under. The big concern of course is that if we all or at least if most of us do not smarten up, things will get a lot worse. I suspect that this is why you have chosen to read this book.

Our ailments have been large and growing in the past eight years. Taxes are still too high; elected officials are out of touch; government is too big; spending is out of control; the new healthcare program is a train wreck; the federal government is incompetent; the people have no voice in government; too many people are too lazy to hold government accountable; too many officials are on the take, and worse than that, the list of ailments is growing, not shortening.

Your intention no doubt in learning about the structure of America and its most fundamental laws, especially the Bill of Rights in choosing to read this book is to help you understand why all this is happening. Thank you. That is why my dad wrote this book. This book is fundamental to understanding your basic rights. From the founding. I am betting that more sooner than later, you will better understand our great country and our great form of government—at least before the bad guys take it away.

This book is the best starter book for anybody wanting to know how things really are and at the same time to refresh their knowledge or learn about the government of the United States of America. Those wanting to be better prepared to react to the over-reach of today's corrupt politicians at the highest levels of government will find this book gives them many answers. Without the knowledge that you can gain easily in this book, for example, you might not understand your rights. Then what?

If you have been paying attention, you know that as a country, we are in trouble. We have a busted economy, high unemployment, no jobs, and our basic rights to freedoms such as speech, religion, the press, and our right-to-bear-arms are being impinged upon. The founders saw it as a civic duty for Americans to pay attention to our government so that we can avoid being chumps and being snookered by crooked politicians.

There are more issues than just those noted above, and we better fix them quickly while we still have a Constitution and a Bill of Rights and a fine new President, upon which to lean.

Black, Yellow, or White, we are on the same side in this battle for the Constitution, the Bill of Rights, and for the survival of America. Together we can all help. We first must understand what is going on and we then must understand our rights as delivered in the Declaration of Independence, The Constitution, and the Bill of

Rights. This book focuses on The Bill of Rights as written as a set of amendments to our Constitution.

My concern is that when we all wake up from our deep fog, there may be no Bill of Rights or Constitution left for our progeny. We will have blown it for sure if that is permitted to happen.

In this book, Brian W. Kelly unabashedly recommends that we stop trusting government since it is clearly not working for our best interests. The sooner we can understand the threat from the left, the sooner we can move on to solving the problem for our values, our country, and our freedom.

The smarter we are, the more chance we have for success. Understanding America's founding and the founding documents, especially the Constitution and The Bill of Rights, is a sure way to become an American forever. I know you love America as I do.

Your author continually monitors what is happening to our government and he has written extensively on the major problems our country faces. Brian W. Kelly is one of America's most outspoken and eloquent conservative spokesmen. He is the author of *The Founding of America, The Constitution by Hamilton, Jefferson, and Madison, Sol Bloom's Epoch Story of the Constitution, No Amnesty! No Way!, Saving America, Taxation Without Representation, Kill the EPA!, Jobs! Jobs! Jobs!, and The Federalist Papers* by the Framers, as well as many other patriotic books. All books are available at amazon.com/author/brianwkelly.

Like many Americans, Brian W Kelly, my dad, is fed up with stifling socialist progressive Marxists in the top seats in Washington. They place the needs of everybody else in front of the needs of Americans. Like many Americans, Kelly is shocked at how brazen the prior administration was in ignoring our Constitution and our Bill of Rights! This had to be stopped. In November 2016, the threats ended. We are all pleased with the new president's actions so far and we ask his fellow Republicans in Congress to get on the stick and make sure you support our President or you will be gone soon.

Brian W. Kelly has read the founding documents, the underlying intelligence reports, and he has researched and written about such topics for years. Brian has written one hundred twenty-six books and hundreds of patriotic articles. He is deeply concerned about how intolerable the results of poor government policy can be within our neighborhoods and our lives. His comprehensible and sane recommendations in this book are explained in detail within the covers of this soon-to-be classic edition.

You are going to love this book, designed by an American for Americans. Few books are must-read but *The Bill of Rights by Founder James Madison* will quickly be at the top of America's most read list.

Sincerely,

Brian P. Kelly, Editor

I am Brian W. Kelly's son

Table of Contents

About the Author

Brian W. Kelly retired as an Assistant Professor in the Business Information Technology (BIT) program at Marywood University, where he also served as the IBM i and midrange systems technical advisor to the IT faculty. Kelly has designed, developed, and taught many college and professional courses. He is also a contributing technical editor to a number of IT industry magazines, including "The Four Hundred" and "Four Hundred Guru" published by IT Jungle. On the Patriotic side, you once could find a patriotic Kelly article at www.conservativeactionalerts.com. This site no longer functions but the articles are still hosted at www.brianwkelly.com

Kelly is a former IBM Senior Systems Engineer and he has been a candidate for US Congress and the US Senate from Pennsylvania. He has an active information technology consultancy. He is the author of 67 books and numerous articles. Kelly is a frequent speaker at National Conferences, and other technical conferences. Ask him to speak at your next TEA Party rally! You might be surprised!

Over the past twenty years, Brian Kelly has become one of America's most outspoken and eloquent conservative protagonists. Besides The Bill of Rights 4 Dummmies, America 4 Dummmies, and The Constitution 4 Dummmies, Kelly is also the author of No Amnesty! No Way!, Taxation Without Representation, and many other patriotic books. Books are available at www.amazon.com/author/brianwkelly

Endorsed by the Independence Hall Tea Party in 2010, Kelly, a Democrat, ran for Congress against a 13-term Democrat and, took no campaign contributions, spent enough to buy signs and T-shirts, and as a virtual unknown, he captured 17% of the vote—www.briankellyforcongress.com. Kelly then supported Republican challenger Lou Barletta, a conservative leader on immigration policy, and helped him win a resounding victory in the general election.

Chapter 1 Americans Are Mad as Hell about Dwindling Rights!

Is your job to give up your rights to others?

Today Americans on the left and the right are being asked to give up their rights so that others, who are jealous of those rights, can be made happy. Today's government leaders in both parties lean left and love to call themselves progressives. Being a progressive today gives some American rights that the founders never dreamed anybody would need or want.

For example, a progressive has the right to lie up a storm and he or she has the right to expect the corrupt media to swear that their word is the Gospel. A progressive can always say they did not take the cookie from the jar, even if their finger prints are all over the jar, and Lieutenant Columbo is saying: "Oh, oh, one more thing, before I forget..."

The point is that liberal progressives seem to have more rights than reality can imagine—including the rights to lie, cheat, and steal with impunity, especially if the real victim is a conservative.

The media enjoys covering for any lefty that lies. The low information crowd (LIC) has lost the ability to discern a lie from the truth. Therefore, lies do not affect the likeability or the electability of a politician. By the way, LICs cannot even discern the meaning of the word discern. That's why our country is in trouble. LICs brag about their lack of knowledge on most subjects when interviewed on the late-night TV celebrity road trips. But their dumbness is not really funny.

We live in a world in which real scandals are mocked as fake scandals and late-night TV hosts are supposedly the only ones who can tell a real scandal from a "fake scandal."

Some of the scandals about which we have learned from government and media sources are in the fake variety according to official government sources.

For the longest time, a sure way to throw off the LICs so they would always lean left was to blame Bush for everything imaginable. Ironically, now with Trump as the President, even the Bushes are blaming the new President and they have given the left a pass.

I do not want to be disrespectful to the institution of the US Presidency. Yet, many of us recall that when cornered, President Obama often said that he got his news from the newspapers, not the White House Daily Briefing. Charles Krauthammer, a paraplegic who still has one of the sharpest mind on the planet, found this a bit problematic. These are his words:

Every now and then, a Hollywood guy goes off the farm or as some say: "*off the reservation*," and insists on telling a new truth, which most often makes the old lies look like they too are true. It is a great trick and it can deliver a lot of laughs in Hollywood if delivered properly. Moreover, it can make the lefties seem smart at times.

Some elitists may say that only those Americans who are really stupid are unaware that the former president was really mad as hell that such things as what he called "the fake scandals" could actually happen. They also suggest that this president would get even "madder" when he had to read the newspaper to find out about the fake scandals as his advisors seemed to want to concentrate on real scandals. They "knew" he is working hard to make everything better—working really hard because he loves America deeply and his love of America is shared equally with, ahem, the First Lady. OK, maybe this paragraph was all fake.

Our country's former president, our one-time CEO, the leader of the free world, would have gladly served in Vietnam but was too young (just six years old) and at the time, unfortunately, he was also living in a Muslim Country (Indonesia), but not as a Muslim, though attending a Muslim school. Regardless of his tender age, they would not have released him for military duty anyway. I think.

At the time, being six years old was not the major reason for the former to not have been able to serve America in Vietnam. As an aside, the largest Muslim population in any country is in Indonesia, but of course that does not cast any aspersions upon anybody mentioned in this chapter.

The Leader of the free world before 2017, wanted all Americans to believe that he had the best intentions and regardless of the crisis du jour, or as the Republicans would call it, the "scandal du jour," he would use his patented formula, which he developed from his substantial personal experience in the free world. "He will study the situation and take the most appropriate action—but only when the time is right." Who could want for more?

Just as the leader of the Free World, our former president, I too am mad as hell about a government that permitted America to be demeaned by either incompetence or intentional efforts towards its destruction.

However, this is not the purpose of this book, though government lies do limit all of our rights that are enumerated in the Bill of Rights and the Constitution. It is however, the underlying truth about why I wrote the book. Would it not be nice if we all told the truth—especially if the truth tellers were high ranking government officials?

In case you missed it in one of my recent books, we're going to offer a scenario from a movie similarly in this book, but we will quickly get on to the meat of the US Bill of Rights, the precious adjunct to the most wonderful document other than the Bible itself—written by the hand of God. I speak of course of the US Constitution.

In essence, Americans are upset today because our Constitution is under attack, and the Constitution is the framework that enables our Bill of Rights. As most historians, and those who studied sixth grade history once knew, the Bill of Rights enumerates specific rights for Americans above and beyond the general rights for all US citizens, which are provided in the US Constitution.

The Constitution which is the big boss over the Bill of Rights says that any rights not so enumerated in the Constitution belong to the people, not the government. Think about that. It means that the government aka, a rogue president such as our past president could not legally countermand any piece of the Constitution, including any of its amendments. Of course, our past president did so anyway by operating illegally and the Congress did not challenge him.

Today's government officials as we all know, unfortunately seem to see it differently. By the time you finish this book, you will have no sympathy for them.

The Constitution—the law of the land—the basis for the Bill of Rights, which you are about to explore in depth, has unlawfully been surpassed by opportunists today in government. That makes a lot of US "Mad as Hell!"

Howard Beale in the paragraphs below represents all frustrated Americans. His story, though unrelated to the theme in the book, really captures the mood and the emotions of America today regarding a government gone wild! *Wild* in this case is a synonym for *"bad."*

You may not remember because you are probably not old enough, but you will like this story regardless. Many of you do have enough life mileage to have seen the movie we now discuss long after its debut in 1976.

Back in November 1976 Howard Beale, as played by Peter Finch, the long-time anchor in the "Hollywood" movie "Network News," gets the bad news that eventually causes him to utter one of the most famous movie lines of all time.

Beale gets fired and is given two weeks. The long-time anchor has a very poor reaction to this news and he cannot control himself during the next news broadcast. You get the feeling that he saw his perceived "rights" being violated.

He feels he is penned in and cannot move forward. With a minimal amount of thought, he promises to commit suicide on the air. The company therefore, immediately fires him—no second chances for a repeat performance.

Beale is naturally devastated and remorseful. He begs for the opportunity to say good-by to his fans with dignity, and his producers think it might be good for the show so they give him his last opportunity ever for air time so that he can say his good-by's to his public and also apologize. He gets his chance

Yet, once on the air, the one-time network news anchorman is overwhelmed by his continuing circumstance. He goes into another diatribe starting off with a rant claiming that "Life is bullshit." He is so passionate that his ratings spike as he persuades his viewers to shout out of their windows: "I'm as mad as hell, and I'm not going to take this anymore!" That is the line heard 'round the world.

Well, my fellow Americans, I bet you saw this coming, and I am going to deliver it as passionately in words as I can: "Like you, I am mad as hell, and I am not going to take this anymore." I know you are too. No more corruption! Let me remind you. Besides one rights violation by government after another, there are the usual issues, but those issues are far worse today than ever before in our country's history. Now that we are mad as hell, we know what we must do.

We the people must continue to smarten up and never be chumps for corrupt politicians. Your job like mine is to keep reading great books about your rights. Stop trusting government and begin to pay attention at all times so we know what the scalawags at the top are up to. Finally, we need to do what we must to replace these the bums in office with solid American citizens.

Chapter 2 The USA is a Constitutional Republic!

A Representative Democracy

We have set the table well for this chapter. We now know that the United States is a suffering giant with caretakers who care more about their personal bank accounts than the people they represent.

None of us, even when we decide to act to save the nation, can do well in defending America without having facts at our disposal. Understanding the Constitution which grants every right to the people except for a few select rights to government such as building an army for defense and maintaining interstate highways, and regulating commerce between the states, and very few others, helps us know that we the people own America, not *it* the government.

My sister Nancy, a very bright person four grades ahead of me taught me the meaning of the word, redundant. We have a phenomenal Bill of Rights formed as the first ten changes to our Constitution, which provide things like freedom of speech, religion, and a bunch of other rights including the right to bear arms.

The irony here is that the explicit Bill of Rights are redundant as all the rights in the Bill of Rights are provided implicitly in the Constitution itself. How is this? Simply by granting the people all rights other than those explicitly granted to the government. The default is that such rights are denied to the government.

Nonetheless, extrinsically pronouncing these rights in the Bill of Rights made a lot of early Americans comfortable with the new government and today they make a lot of us comfortable that the government cannot pretend to have any of the rights deemed specifically for the people.

Other good stuff in the Constitution

The Constitution prescribes that the US is a representative democracy, which as you probably already know means that because we have an elected chief executive (president) and a constitution, it makes our country a *republic*. A republic is a better deal for all Americans than simply a democracy.

Most of us know the pledge of allegiance, which was once mandatory to recite daily in US schools at the beginning of the school day. However, at that time there was no question about whether our government believed that Americans should love America.

The "Pledge" contains the words: "…and to the *Republic* for which it stands." Our great, and wonderful and rightfully proud country is thus both a representative democracy and a republic.

When we think of the very important notion that "America is a representative democracy," watching the "clowns" from both parties, who occupy our central government, it is a sane question to ask if this is really true.

The song, "Is that all there is?" comes to my mind. We are nothing like our parents and nothing like our founders. We have reason to be ashamed of our corrupt government, but then again, our country today is so far off the founders' mark that even shame cannot squeeze in under the line as being politically correct.

Our representative democracy is the foundation of America. However, what makes America—America is that we are also a republic—the finest form of government ever brought forth from mankind. The Bill of Rights, the main curative subject for corruption in this book is just an add-on to an unending list of inalienable rights for the people—you and me.

The part that those not educated in civics, like the youth of our times and the know-it-all millennials, do not understand is that government has no rights under the constitution other than those specifically granted by the people. Government also has no money and no resources other than the taxes they steal from regular Americans.

Government is not the answer. If it were any kind of answer it would deliver poorly on your expectations. Government was set up to be the people's slave but there are people looking for gifts from its own slave labor given to the government. They have given the government far greater powers than the constitutional democracy (republic) permits.

Thus, when the government goes awry as today, it must be reined in. But, you already know that as you are one of the chosen to read this book about your rights as a citizen of the USA. Those who do not know this are prepared to permit this country to be ruled by the government for the government and let the people be damned!

America has a great set of laws, beginning with our Constitution, the primary law of the land. These laws govern all people and all politicians in perpetuity—as long as *we* choose to hold our politicians (aka elected officials) accountable.

The fact that we Americans no longer hold our officials accountable is why they are not accountable. It is our fault. We get the government we deserve as we look for favors from scummy, filthy, dirty politicians and scalawags, when in fact it is they who owe allegiance to us in our role of "we the people."

What is a republic?

To answer the first unasked question first, let me say "No!" You do not have to be a Republican to live in a republic. Forget about political party labels. The founders brought forth America and expressly forbade the inclusion of political parties in our government. Republican and Democrat are identifying terms to political parties that evolved over many years in America. They could just as easily be called Party 1 and Party 2 and their meaning would be the same.

Republicans have nothing to do with a republic and Democrats have nothing to do with a democracy. When we come to grips that the type of democracy that we have is for all the people from all parties and it is a constitutional democracy (having a constitution), that makes it a republic. That's that! A democracy with a constitution, a set of basic laws, is a republic, even if it consists of people, none of which are

Republican. It is also a constitutional represented Democracy, even if it consists of people none of which are not Democrats.

The simple definition of a republic (from Latin -- res publica), is as follows: a state in which supreme power is held by the people and their elected representatives, and which has an elected or nominated president rather than a monarch.

That is us folks. As long as we believe that, we should also believe that neither the Congress nor a President no matter how loved by Democrats or Republicans can violate the Constitution by executing laws that have never been passed by the legislature. President Obama admitted this and then violated his very own words on multiple occasions. That is pure corruption.

In practice in a republic, the government is ruled by elected leaders run according to law. The law in our country is called **The Constitution**. Unlike a democracy, a republic is not based only on majority rule. The law of the land, a Constitution which contains a set of dos and don'ts gives the minority a voice.

Moreover, the majority cannot decide in such a government that Brian W. Kelly, your humble author, can be summarily executed since he does not measure up to the majority's expectations. The Constitution does not permit such vile action. In a republic, it takes lots more than that and that is why real laws are important to us all.

Our biggest and most important laws within the US Constitution are written so that the government cannot hurt US or impose its will upon US without our explicit consent. Our country was founded by some very smart people and they knew that without constraints on any government, which could potentially go wild, the people could not and thus, would not win.

The constraints in the Constitution are implicit in that all of the rights are owned by the people, and only those rights explicitly given to government are for the government. The only purpose of the Bill of Rights is so that Americans know where their starter set of rights begin. Government has no additional rights.

Let me repeat. Government has no rights other than those granted by law to the government by the people. The people have all the rights. A government that subjugates the people for its purposes is expressly forbidden in these United States of America.

This great body of law known as the Constitution therefore makes politicians and others in government fear a backlash when they attempt to deny the people, even just one person, our liberty and freedom. In a pure democracy, if the majority decided that you or I should be killed, nothing would necessarily stop it if it were to be. But, in a republic such as ours, it is the rule of law which prevails and the rule of law starts with the Constitution. Many of our elected officials at all levels of government today do not understand the minimal authority of the government. Nobody and no government can determine that a person can be killed unless it has been a determination of the courts. Majorities can kill nobody.

It seems for sure that many in our nation today, mostly on the far left, are trying really hard to kill America's America by demeaning the Constitution and the Bill of Rights in particular. With majority rule in a pure democracy, the only problem is that you may not be in the majority. Then what?

You more than likely selected this book to help fight off those who do not respect our fundamental laws. If the courts stay honest, and that is not assured, the people will always prevail because the laws are on our side.

If you could figure any way to put an unmovable grip on corrupt politicians, right now or in the future, would you not do so? The founders of America put such a stranglehold on all political agents of the future when they wrote and adopted the US Constitution, the greatest body of law ever written in any civilization. Government has no inalienable rights. Such rights are reserved for the people, and many of those rights are explicitly listed in the Bill of Rights!

The problem of course is that government administers public things such as cities, states, and federal agencies as well as the "public" schools. But, the people are the masters of government at all levels as well as the public schools. This matters not one iota if the people do not understand they are the masters and not the slaves. If officials do not follow the law, the people must step in to stop the perpetration.

However, if we the people do not know what is written in the Constitution, or the Bill of Rights, it cannot help America too much. Can it? So, it is time for all Americans who have not been paying attention to stop being dummies, political sport (chumps) for the elite. It is time to rule America as our birthright as citizens of this great country commands US to do. Let somebody else eat cake!

And, so, my fellow Americans, that is the number one reason that in order to form a more perfect union of the original thirteen colonies / states, and with more states expected after the first thirteen, our forefathers built the finest Constitution ever fashioned by a pen in human hands.

The Bible, from the hand of God, may be the greatest story ever told in the greatest book ever written, but the Constitution is as good as it gets for the goodness of man, written by the hands of our first patriots. Surely, this document was written with the guidance of God.

In this day and age, there are everyday attempts by the government, which is controlled by the far left on the ideology spectrum, to undermine our lasting republic, which is an almost pure constitutional representative democracy. As noted, the attacks most often come from the left side of the political spectrum, which is the side that would in a heartbeat would replace our Constitution with books written by Marx and Engels.

Democracy is the opposite of communism

You would doubt me only if you knew nothing of our founding and the anti-people notions of Marx and Engels. The ideology of the progressive left today, masquerading as the Democrat Party, along with the corrupt press favor Marxism in its simpler forms of socialism and communism.

Since Americans do not as a rule vote for socialists, communists, or Marxists, these are things that nobody other than a crooked politician would want. Even though far left politicians desire these ends, they will not openly speak about the socialist or communistic state which they espouse because they have not duped the people enough. So, to a large extent the people would resist but the persistent left is wearing many Americans down.

If you are unaware of this in today's government, I would recommend that you consider paying more attention. No politician wanting to be elected will admit that they are more communist than American. Yet, as much as it pains me to tell you, unfortunately, they are!

The overtures, which demean the Constitution, the fabric of our democracy, originate from corrupt politicians who have been caught up in the leftist movement, which would like to end capitalism, and bring on a socialist / communist order in which they were the leaders. They want to replace the American Dream, and all the dreams of *We the People*! And they would love it to happen so they could be our leaders in a communist world without having to fire a shot.

The people have the responsibility of keeping government honest!

Most of the time in our great form of government, we can sit back and let other good people govern for us. What happens if they begin to govern for their own selfish interests? The founders thought this might happen They did not suggest that Americans sit on the couch and let this happen. They fought a revolution against old England so America would continue to be free and ruled by the people.

They founded a country in which it was up to all the people to understand our laws—first the Constitution, of which the Bill of Rights is key, and then to pay attention so that our leaders follow those laws. After having fought a revolution for freedom, the early Americans were not about to let those who opposed their desire for freedom to retake America and force another war of independence.

When today, our supposed dedicated leaders do not follow the laws of the land, we must learn to send them home every two, four, or six years, as determined by the term lengths as set forth in Constitution for our House (2 years), the President (4 years), and the Senate (6 years) respectively. Corrupt representatives do not deserve a second chance.

To say it more clearly: We get to throw the bums out and replace them with people of character on a regular basis. Don't give up; vote them out!

With the people in control our government has been able to work well for over 240 years. When we get bad apples, we must throw them away by voting them out. Of course, that means we must always vote in order for our choices to matter.

Representatives are to be of the people?

Though representatives are supposed to come from the people, a type of political class of elites has come about and seldom do we get to vote for representatives anymore—who are truly of the people. Groups of politicians and special interests in the same party group together to determine who gets their money and who will ultimately get the nomination. John Doe might as well not take a shot unless a lot of other John Doe's provide big help.

By understanding America better, and especially by understanding our Constitution and its built-in Bill of Rights, Americans have a far better chance of bringing good and honest government back to the people.

The way it now currently works, there is far too much separation between US, the electors, and them, the elected officials. Most officials choose to live in gated communities, unaware of what is happening on our streets in our communities with regular joes.

The Constitution provides that our elected officials are given the task to coordinate our pooled resources for the intended benefit of "everyone." Everyone is this country until recently meant all US citizens. But everyone is often not included? We see politicians taking credit for spending treasury dollars on things that simply buy themselves votes. Nobody wants this and so it is up to all of US—we the people—to change it.

Like Gary Hart said so well in a great essay he wrote in 2015, our government is wholly unaccountable to w*e the people t*oday. The government rejects the fundamental principles of our founding and has no real legitimacy the further it drifts from the precepts of the Constitution.

The US was not designed for a government of the government by the government and for the government. The Constitution is the blueprint for our country's design. It was designed by a group of founding artisans to not only represent their artistic touch, but to be held as the behavioral creed of the people, for the people, and by the people, forever. What thinking human being blessed to be part of America, could ask for anything more?

If you think that life, freedom, liberty, property, and the ability to pursue your own happiness are simple notions, and *givens* in any civilization, get out your thinking cap, and think again. Why do people from all over the world crash our gates just to get in? The US is an exceptional country.

As a point of note, Rush Limbaugh, who is a great patriot, has a great explanation of American exceptionalism. "American exceptionalism is about the exception to the rule or the exception to the norm, not that we're better people, not that we have better DNA, not that we're smarter. We've had more freedom. We've had more liberty. Obama doesn't understand that."

Americans are exceptional in that we have full freedom and liberty in our country, and with that we can exceed all limits of ordinary expectation. Go to any other country, and this exception no longer applies.

Throughout our short history, the USA has been the freest nation in the world with rights withheld from government and rights given to the people by our Constitution and given specifically by the Bill of Rights.

Today as our country's foundation is being threatened from within, more than likely you are reading about the Bill of Rights and the Constitution so that you can extrapolate your American rights from this mélange of patriotic writings. When you finally get it and you understand your rights, you will then guard and protect your rights as well as work hard to protect this great nation, which provides them. It really is that simple.

If you had to give some rights up—which of your rights would you first give up? Your freedom? Your life? Your liberty? Your family? Your property? Or would you give up your ability to do what you needed to do to be happy? The sanest answer of course is "none of the above."

Who could ask for anything more than being an American? Ask the last arriving immigrant why they come here! We are free! But, if Americans do not care about our founding precepts to protect them from scoundrels, maybe our freedom, our lives, our liberty, our families, and our ability to do what we need to be happy, will be taken from us one day—perhaps in the not-too-distant future Maybe most of our rights lost over the last eight years, are already gone.

If the design of our nation, America, which the founders labored to create is so great, you might ask, why is it that our current lawmakers ignore it? Why are they so nefarious? Elected lawmakers have no trouble going with the flow and committing US to years of debt without even taking the time to read the debt-ridden legislation for which they vote. Neither the Constitution nor the Bill of Rights founders permitted today's Americans to bill future generations for the bills due today. Likewise, our public officials have no such rights. Our founders would not approve of what our representatives, including our past President for eight years, have done to our country.

Even worse, members of Congress, our alleged civil servants, the supposed representatives of the people, without even sweating, can get away without doing their jobs. At the same time, they are collecting more and more remuneration for their main act of either dallying or passing legislation for special interests, thus hurting the American people at large.

The true answer to that question [Why is it that our current lawmakers ignore the laws of the nation?] is very unfortunate for Americans. There is tacit collaboration in undermining the principles of our Democratic Republic by our supposed representatives, their supporters, the press, the special interests, lobbyists, and their corporate interests.

We the people now come last. They think we are not paying attention. Maybe we have not been paying enough attention but don't you agree that—that is about to end. *Pay attention* is about to become the motto of the free in America! Let the subjugated wish for more government! Let the free actively seek to keep our freedom and liberty!

Amen!

Chapter 3 Bill of Rights Says: Throws the Bums Out!

Write opinion letters and call your representatives

The purpose of this book as noted from the beginning is to keep America as founded and to help US all be better Americans by understanding the Bill of Rights, an essential ingredient of the US Constitution. At the same time, as an adjunct to a greater understanding of our rights, we all need to learn a lot about America's founding. Most of us have heard of the Bill of Rights as an integral part of the US Constitution and when our rights are presented properly, we really like them. Who could say no to prosperity through liberty and freedom?

Many know the story of the Bill of Rights as it was actually an after-thought to the US Constitution—the defining document of our country. Doubtful patriots, who examined the Constitution for approval, wrote that all powers and rights not explicitly given to the government were held by the people. That means that the people own the government and not vice versa. So, let's say among other specific powers, the Constitution grants to the President, the Congress, and the Courts operating as the government the following powers / rights:

- ✓ To lay and collect import duties
- ✓ To pay the debts of the U.S. Government.
- ✓ To regulate commerce with foreign nations and Indian Tribes.
- ✓ To regulate commerce among the States.
- ✓ To regulate immigration
- ✓ To build roads and bridges
- ✓ To provide for the common defense (Army, Navy…), E
- ✓ Etc.

As you can see, these are things that we all would expect government to do as well as a number of other specific tasks all laid out in the Constitution. As you read the Constitution for free on the Internet or by a book by this author, you will notice that certain rights for government are not included; such as:

- ✓ Killing Citizens.
- ✓ Preventing the people from assembling in groups of more than two.
- ✓ Demanding that the people shop only at government stores.
- ✓ Requiring men to shave
- ✓ Preventing the people from eating on Tuesday.
- ✓ Etc.

This quote from the Tenth Amendment of the Bill of Rights applies regarding government powers as follows:

The powers not delegated to the United States by the Constitution, nor prohibited by it to the States, are reserved to the States respectively, or to the people.

Only the rights specifically given to government in the Constitution are in government's purview. All other rights are reserved for the people. In other words, the people have all other powers and rights than those specifically given to government. Don't be fooled otherwise.

Any power not listed in the Constitution specifically, says the Tenth Amendment, is left to the states or the people. Although the Tenth Amendment does not specify what these "powers" may be, the U.S. Supreme Court has ruled that laws affecting family relations (such as marriage, divorce, and adoption), commerce that occurs within a state's own borders, and local law enforcement activities, are among those specifically reserved to the states or the people.

Since the Constitution gives almost all rights and powers to the people, there was disagreement among many of the founders and the citizens of the 1780's about the Constitution outlining specifically all the rights of the people. There was a difference of opinion and the Bill of Rights ultimately arrived after the Constitution was ratified to clarify the intent of the founders on the matter of government powers and state's rights.

The majority of the founders believed that by saying the people have all rights other than those reserved for government, as they wrote in The Constitution, and the government had only those rights specifically mentioned, that should have been enough. What more should we have needed?

To repeat, the Constitution as written from the beginning already provided all rights the people would ever put in a Bill of Rights, and the government was given its specific powers so it could function as a government.

Though this is not how it actually works, let's try this exercise to get a better understanding of our rights v. government rights.

Rather than saying the people have all rights not explicitly granted by the people to the government, let's suppose that the founders tried to define every single right / power for all Americans. In this process, let's say they numbered the rights beginning with number 1.

Suppose when all the rights were listed and added to the Constitution, the number of rights was calculated to be, say, 437. What would happen if in trying to define the 437 rights, which in this scenario the founders believed all Americans should possess, they forgot a right or just a part of right? Then what? What if this particular right's number just happened to be 93? Then what?

In this fictitious scenario of 437 rights and no more, to make our point, as noted, the Constitution as written provides not just for right number 93, but all rights from zero to 437 but no additional rights. Anything beyond 437 if listed would be a power of the government by default. Again, this is a fictitious example but the point is that this could have been an alternative way of granting rights that would be very specific with numbered rights and no global rights permitted.

To clarify further, the people in this fictitious scenario did not have global rights. They had all rights defined from zero to 437 but none others and no parts that were forgotten and not specified. Anything that was forgotten in a specific right was not a right.

To say again, anything that would be a right of the people would have to be specified within the 437 defined rights or it would not be a right / power of the people. Government would have its listed powers and rights as well as discussed above but rights not listed for the people would be in the government column. Does that sound better than the people having all the rights except those they place in the government's column?

As you might suspect, there would be a problem when a missing right were needed, once the Constitution was finalized. The problem would occur when the people sought to have a right number 438, about which nobody ever would have conceived when the rights were originally numbered to 437?

What if enough people were pro-government that they would not vote the people to have the additional rights or to have right # 93 amended to add the forgotten clause? It could create a big problem for the people. It would give the government the greater hand over the people's hand.

It helps to remember that the founders in forming the US government are the same group that seceded from England because England had all the rights. They fought a revolution to gain all the rights that were natural for the people to possess. They were not about to give government any loopholes in which government could claim power over the people that were not fully intended by the founders.

And, so the default is that the states, aka the people, got the rights and the federal government got the enumerated powers—only those powers specifically listed in the Constitution.

So, what did the founders do so there would not be conflicts of new rights or parts of rights that were not specifically noted? at this would never happen?

1. The constitution specifically lists all of government's rights / powers.
2. All other rights are granted to the people.

3. A Bill of Rights was added to the Constitution for the people—though the Bill of rights is redundant since the Constitution already grants all rights not reserved for government to the people.

4. Since a new right is already granted by the Constitution, rights do not have to be granted specifically and were not often granted after the Bill of Rights was devised and ratified.

5. Despite this great compromise, only ten of the twelve rights proposed were ratified; and since that time, just seventeen changes were made to the constitution in the form of amendments—the same form in which the Bill of Rights were presented.

The Constitution and its 27 amendments including the Bill of Rights is the place to go to find out what America is all about! It is about the U.S. of A.—our nation. Our Country is what it is because its definition is embodied in its Constitution, which is America's most fundamental prized set of laws. The Bill of Rights and all other Constitutional changes (amendments) together with the base Constitution represent the total body of the Constitution.

To say it again for clarity, all amendments to the Constitution, especially the first ten known as the Bill of Rights, are in fact part of the Constitution. They are not adjuncts to it in function; though they are in form. And thus, the Bill of Rights, the topic of this book is a major part of the Constitution. It is not a bunch of independent precepts brought forth to make us all feel better about life.

Our job, as Americans moving through life of course, is to learn what we can about our government (as defined by the Constitution—including the Bill of Rights et al.). In this endeavor, we should all pay attention that our Congressional representatives actually spend their time representing US according to the laws of the founders, who, if they had their way, would never let US down.

When our representatives do not do the will of the people in-between elections we must remember that they represent US, not the government. We need to write letters to the editors of newspapers and other media, and write our Congressmen and Senators so they know they cannot snooker us, and so they know who is the boss—we the people.

If they don't listen, then we must do the honorable thing and write them even more letters, and letters to the editors of popular newspapers, and if and when they choose not to respond in our favor, or worse than that, they do not respond at all, we then must un-elect these leaders their next time out on the ballot.

Un-elect them! They would hate it!

Unfortunately for Americans, our representative in the Congress, the Supreme Court, and the Presidency is not Jefferson Smith from the movie *Mr. Smith Goes to Washington*. His honor is impeccable. But, the honor of our representatives in the twenty-first century has become very tarnished and quite questionable.

Do they represent US or do they represent themselves? Do they represent corporations or special interests? If our representatives are doing their jobs, why is our country messed up so badly that it may be irreparable as Congress cannot or will not work together for the good of the people.

When our country is handed over to non-citizens by our representatives, have they represented the citizens of the USA? When a president addresses unescorted children from Central America and he tells them they are the future of America, what is he really telling the children of American citizens?

Our representation has been getting progressively worse each year—not better. Over the past few years, especially from 2009 through 2016, with the healthcare debacle and open borders topping the list of domestic travails, it is clear that the voices of the people were not being heard in Washington, DC.

The government of the past administration seemingly every day weakened our opportunity to survive as it cut and health services that we need and then it cut again. None of us want a corrupt government deciding if we live or die or what health services we can get or not get.

Government should make no decisions regarding the healthcare of an individual person.

Just as Jefferson Smith in the Frank Capra classic movie, *Mr. Smith Goes to Washington*, found out, the corrupt purposes of elected officials are now in the open. It is to serve themselves by serving special interests. During the past administration, government officials have been emboldened to steal away rights from the people to better suit the government.

Because government does not have the right or the power to do this, these recent actions have been unconstitutional. Simply by being unconstitutional does not fix the usurpation of power. Instead, the government making such bad choices must be replaced by a government that will reinstate the power of the people. And. The people's ultimate power is to replace representation that has gone bad.

In the sunlight of the day, therefore, the existing Congress—yes, both houses, must go. Not the institution of Congress, just the corrupt members who choose not to serve the people.

We must bid them sayonara. We must say adieu. We must sign off with a big adios. Our right to do this comes directly from the Constitution, not from the Bill of Rights—but the Tenth Amendment emphasizes the rights of all Americans to run America. It is a right of all Americans to un-elect the scoundrels that rip our country apart.

And when it comes time to elect our next President, and our next Congress; let's not forget to bring in an honest person who loves America as much as we do. Many feel that President Donald Trump fits that description but Congress still has not yet gotten the people's message. If the mess we had during the past president's tenure, if it were not the president's intentions, and the president's direct fault, then whose fault, I might ask, was it?

Might it have been Stanley Laurel's or Oliver Hardy's—for it surely is a comedy!! It was President Barack H. Obama and he is gone, and many of us say, Thank God! Others of course miss his unconstitutional executive orders. But, they are not friends of an America created by our founders.

I was very surprised. As we examine the notions that come our way, isn't that why you are reading this book? Thank you to all the Americans ready to fight for American values. We need more of you today in our America! "Don't give up the ship." Keep firing until America wins.

You may know that about a year into the War of 1812, the first full scale war for the new America after the Revolution, Captain James Lawrence said these heroic words after being mortally wounded. It was in the engagement between his ship, the U.S. frigate Chesapeake, and the HMS Shannon on June 1, 1813. While the wounded Lawrence was being carried below, his duty for his ship and his love for America motivated him to order his officers: "Tell the men to fire faster! Don't give up the ship!"

Keep firing until America wins. Use the Bill of Rights, the Constitution, and all great American principles as your ammunition.

Chapter 4 The US Constitution

Introduction to the Constitution

The founders were mainly pleased with the Constitution as a more perfect union than the Articles of Confederation. Those who wrote the Articles of Confederation admitted its imperfections not too long after its ratification. It was an imperfect constitution for the newly formed union but far better than having no law of the land.

The Congress read the Letters of Delegates to Congress, which contained drafts of the Articles of Confederation, written by Josiah Bartlett and John Dickinson from late June 1776. Both Bartlett and Dickinson were members of the committee tasked with writing the draft of the Articles of Confederation.

Let's review the adoption of the Articles of Confederation before we move directly to the Constitution. After fine tuning the drafts presented in the Letters, The Continental Congress adopted the Articles of Confederation, the first constitution of the United States, on November 15, 1777.

However, ratification of the Articles of Confederation by all thirteen states did not occur until March 1, 1781. The Articles created a loose confederation of sovereign states and a weak central government, leaving most of the power with the state governments. The need for a stronger Federal government soon became apparent and eventually led to the Constitutional Convention in 1787. The present United States Constitution replaced the Articles of Confederation on March 4, 1789.

To put the Constitution in proper perspective, we can ask ourselves if it would have been possible for Bill Gates to have introduced Windows 10 in 1985 rather than Windows 1.0? That answer is a clear no.

Mr. Gates and Microsoft needed to go through all of the versions from Windows 1.0 to Windows 10 to learn what was needed in Windows 10. This is similar to how The Constitution is a better version of the first law of the land, the Articles of Confederation. Once there is a basis for something, it can be improved. As version 1.0, The Articles were well done but needed improvement. A "more perfect union" was necessary. The Constitution represents version 2.0.

The additional features in the Constitution over the Articles of Confederation are substantial. In many ways, it was like going from Windows 1.0 to Windows 98. Then, of course the Bill of Rights was like moving to Windows NT from 98. Now, add in the 17 other constitutional amendments, each a minor update to the Constitution, and we can ask ourselves in Microsoft parlance, "What version of the Constitution are we running today?

As an aside, besides the powers of government being separated, which items gave the government a higher probability for tyranny? George Washington described the biggest problem with the Articles of Confederation in just two words, "no money."

Under the Articles, the Federal government relied on the states for funding. Without the Constitution, America might really be the name of a large land mass with 48 countries, and two not so contiguous countries--Hawaii and Alaska. A country with no money could not survive over the long haul.

The barebones Constitution itself was far more perfect than the Articles of Confederation, just like Windows 98 was far more perfect than Windows 1.0. Microsoft could not immediately go to Windows 10 because nobody knew how any of the other previous versions would behave or be accepted, and all the subsequent iterations of Windows occurred from its use over time, and its technological successes and failings. So, with the Constitution! Besides, for Microsoft, substantially less powerful hardware could run Windows 1.0 fine but would have a coughing spell trying to boot Windows 10.

In many ways, our country grew the same way—in stages. The phrase "a more perfect union," in the Preamble of the Constitution notes the imperfections in a prior version and it introduces the rationale for the drawing of the *Constitution* from the *Articles of Confederation.*

We know from reading the prior chapters that the imperfect document was *The Articles of Confederation.* Bill Gates knew that the prior document to Windows was the last version of DOS without the Windows GUI. He knew he could make it better after he visited Xerox's Palo Alto Research Center and learned about GUI in the mid 1970's.

The U.S. Constitution (and its subsequent 27 amendments) mimics the idea of having a v3.1, V4.1.x, and V5. x.3. It has survived for over well over two-hundred years without many changes. This notion of a basis document and then perfections in subsequent versions testifies to the eventual almost perfection of the Constitution.

Like Windows, it went through multiple iterations to get to The Constitution. Back in 1787, it was built to be the basis of the constitutional representative democracy (Republic) of the United States. If he were alive at the time, even Bill Gates would have approved.

From the National Archives:

http://www.archives.gov/national-archives-experience/charters/constitution.html

I like how this text from the national archives reads—so instead of trying to rephrase this, I have included it below to explain the purpose of the work behind the Constitution. We have heard this before in this book, and so it should ring quite familiar.

> *"The Federal Convention convened in the State House (Independence Hall) in Philadelphia on May 14, 1787, to revise the Articles of Confederation. Because the delegations from only two states were at first present, the members adjourned from day to day until a quorum of seven states was obtained on May 25. [I would bet the adjournments took the quorum-less participants to Philadelphia's historic City Tavern, a fine place even today to libate.] Through discussion and debate it became clear by mid-June that, rather than amend the existing Articles, the Convention would draft an entirely new frame of government.*

The City Tavern, Philadelphia, PA

Best entrance view. Operating since 1773.

"All through the summer, in closed sessions, the delegates debated, and redrafted the articles of the new Constitution. Among the chief points at issue were how much power to allow the central government, how many representatives in Congress to allow each state, and how these representatives should be elected--directly by the people or by the state legislators. The work of many minds, the Constitution stands as a model of cooperative statesmanship and the art of compromise."

The Law of the Land

As noted previously, since 1787, the Constitution of the United States has comprised the primary law of the U.S. Federal Government. In simple terms, it is the law of the land, and all other laws must conform to the statutes contained within this original document and its amendments, from the Bill of Rights to Amendment # 27.

This law also describes the three chief branches of the Federal Government and their jurisdictions as well as the separation of the powers. It also gives the nation the ability to levy taxes, though an income tax was not permitted in the Constitution on people or corporations. Let's take a break and look more closely at the income tax amendment. We'll be back on page 51 to continue our discussion soon.

Ironically, and quite smartly, there was no income tax provision in The Constitution. The founders did not want a personal or corporate income tax mainly because it might be apportioned so that certain states paid more than others to the central government.

The people in the early twentieth century for their own reasons voted to ratify the Sixteenth amendment to the Constitution. This gave the Congress the right to tax them and US, and corporations at a personal level. Dum, Dumm, Dummm, and Dummmer must have been the lawyers representing the people in the campaign for passage of this terrible amendment. In the passage of this law, there was both chicanery and a lot more irony.

As hard as it may be to believe, the Sixteenth Amendment, which gave the American people the misery of confiscatory income taxes, was a trick. It never was supposed to have passed. Good people representing good people would never have permitted it.

It was introduced by the Republicans as part of a political scheme to fake-out the Democrats from a tax increase bill that would have passed but could never have been enforced because it would be unconstitutional. But, the Republican trick backfired.

As previously noted, the Founding Fathers had rejected income taxes (as well as any other direct taxes) in the Constitution unless they were apportioned to each state according to population.

The politicians in the US Senate in the early 1900s passed a bill to institute the Sixteenth Amendment permitting such direct taxation in violation of the founders' intentions. They wanted more largesse to distribute by getting more dollars in the treasury from taxpayers to assure their elections. It was their first grab at redistribution of income.

The people of course would have to ratify such an amendment if it passed Congress. It surprisingly passed unanimously 77-0 in the Senate! The House also approved it by another large margin, 318-14. Nobody was thinking, including the people in the states!

It was then sent to the states for ratification. State after state ratified this "soak the rich" amendment, thinking it would not affect them until it went into full force and effect on February 12, 1913. The people voted to tax the rich but just about everybody has been taxed ever since. You can never outfox a foxy politician. Democratic President Wilson was the best at politics and communism and progressivism, but he was not a very good leader in other ways.

In the Economic Policy Journal in April 2012, David, a blogger, called it right with his opinion of many Americans. His explanation, which is quoted below is that Americans would not vote for somebody, even Ron Paul who they truly believe would eliminate the income tax on everybody, because they think the rich should pay all the taxes and they should pay none. David sees it as a matter of class envy and offers a bleak outlook on the chances of it getting better until people wake up. Let's not be David, please. See what he has to say:

"Americans are envious and covetous of the wealth of others. They don't want freedom. They like a government that will do things to them, so long as the resulting chains appear to be gold plated. They like politicians that stir up class envy. Humans by nature are slaves. They don't yearn to be free, responsible, independent people. Until this wholly selfish and self-centered people awaken from their slumber; and learn to hate their slavery to government, until the iron of their chains eats into their soul, things are going to get worse."

The fact that Americans are beginning to get upset is a good sign. More and more people, like you, the reader, will be looking to learn about their rights and then I predict they will come after government with a vengeance. The times when politicians could survive despite their malfeasance in office are about to end because the people are about to end it. Thank you for reading this book.

I like to repeat to make a point. The fact that good citizens such as you are reading a book about the Bill of Rights is another good sign. I think this will all turn around with the help of some good leaders. That means we Americans must do our best to kick every federal politician (representative) out of office and replace them with good people as soon as we can. Then we take our battle to the state capitals, and then the cities. Finally, America will be run by the people again.

Back to the Constitution

In addition to permitting all but direct taxation, The Constitution lays out the basic rights of citizens of the United States. The Constitution of the United States is the oldest federal constitution in existence in the world, and it was framed by a convention of delegates from twelve of the thirteen original states in Philadelphia in May 1787.

The Constitution is the landmark legal document of the United States and all other laws are tested against its specifications. Many other constitutions, such as the Constitution of Mexico, for example are based on this work.

The text of the entire Constitution is available for free on the Internet as well as hardcopy books for sale in bookstores. Your author's best seller Taxation Without Representation includes Appendices with all of the founding documents mentioned in this book.

The Bill of Rights (first ten amendments) and the other 17 amendments are described in detail in subsequent chapters. There are also a number of Amendments that were submitted but did not pass. This would make interesting reading on the Internet.

The Constitution is a free document for anybody to record and retransmit in any form. It is over two hundred twenty-five years old. It makes America, America.

Summary of the US Constitution

Explanation / Summary of Article I of the US Constitution:

Article I: The Legislative Branch consists of 10 sections and defines:

1. All Legislative powers,
2. Composition of the House of Representatives,
3. Composition of the Senate
4. Holding Elections,
5. Congress sets its own rules by House,
6. Compensation for Senators,
7. Revenue Bills originate in House,
8. Congress can lay and collect taxes,
9. States' rights and taxes,
10. State treaties.

Note: Article I, Section 9, Clause 8 of the Constitution is of particular interest to this writer.

For your convenience, this is provided below:

Section 9 Clause 8: No Title of Nobility shall be granted by the United States: And no Person holding any Office of Profit or Trust under them, shall, without the Consent of the Congress, accept of any present, Emolument, Office, or Title, of any kind whatever, from any King, Prince, or foreign State.

Article II: The Executive Branch: Consists of 4 sections and defines:

(1) Executive Power and President, (2) President as Commander in Chief, (3) State of the Union & Information Requirements, (4) Rules of Executive Branch impeachment

Article III: The Judicial Branch: Consists of 3 sections and defines:

(1) Judicial Power, (2) Laws and Trial by Jury, (3) Treason

Article IV: Relations Between States: Consists of 4 sections and defines:

(1) Faith and Credit of State Laws, (2) Privileges apply to all in all states, (3) New States May be Admitted to the Union, (4) Federal guarantee to defend states.

Article V: The Amendment Process: Consists of 1 section and defines the amendment process for adding / deleting to/from the Constitution.

Article VI: General Provisions, Supremacy of the Constitution: Consists of 1 section and defines the debt process and the requirement to support the Constitution

Article VII: Ratification Process: Consists of 1 section and it outlines the process for ratifying the Constitution.

End of Constitution summary. The full text of the US Constitution is available for free on the Internet.

Chapter 5 The Text of The Bill of Rights

A Charter of Freedom

The Bill of Rights is seen as the third of the three charters of freedom—the pillars of our Republic. Along with the Declaration of Independence and the Constitution, the Bill of Rights defines America. The Bill was granted by the Congress of the United States, begun and held at the City of New-York, on Wednesday the fourth of March, one thousand seven hundred and eighty-nine.

The text of the Bill looks exactly as follows:

THE Conventions of a number of the States, having at the time of their adopting the Constitution, expressed a desire, in order to prevent misconstruction or abuse of its powers, that further declaratory and restrictive clauses should be added; And as extending the ground of public confidence in the Government, will best ensure the beneficent ends of its institution.

RESOLVED by the Senate and House of Representatives of the United States of America, in Congress assembled, two thirds of both Houses concurring, that the following Articles be proposed to the Legislatures of the several States, as amendments to the Constitution of the United States, all, or any of which Articles, when ratified by three-fourths of the said Legislatures, to be valid to all intents and purposes, as part of the said Constitution; viz.

ARTICLES in addition to, and Amendment of the Constitution of the United States of America, proposed by Congress, and ratified by the Legislatures of the several States, pursuant to the fifth Article of the original Constitution.

Article the first. ... After the first enumeration required by the first article of the Constitution, there shall be one Representative for every 30,000 until the number shall amount to 100, after which the proportion shall be so regulated by Congress, that there shall be not less than 100 Representatives, nor less than one Representative for every 40,000 persons, until the number of Representatives shall amount to 200; after which the proportion shall be so regulated by Congress, that there shall not be less than 200 Representatives, nor more than one Representative for every 50,000 persons.

Article the second ... No law, varying the compensation for the services of the Senators and Representatives, shall take effect, until an election of Representatives shall have intervened.

Article the third ... Congress shall make no law respecting an establishment of religion, or prohibiting the free exercise thereof; or abridging the freedom of speech, or of the press; or the right of the people peaceably to assemble, and to petition the Government for a redress of grievances.

Article the fourth ... A well-regulated Militia, being necessary to the security of a free state, the right of the people to keep and bear arms, shall not be infringed.

Article the fifth ... No soldier shall, in time of peace be quartered in any house, without the consent of the owner, nor in time of war, but in a manner to be prescribed by law.

Article the sixth ... The right of the people to be secure in their persons, houses, papers, and effects, against unreasonable searches and seizures, shall not be violated, and no Warrants shall issue, but upon probable cause, supported by Oath or affirmation, and particularly describing the place to be searched, and the persons or things to be seized.

Article the seventh ... No person shall be held to answer for a capital, or otherwise infamous crime, unless on a presentment or indictment of a Grand Jury, except in cases arising in the land or naval forces, or in the Militia, when in actual service in time of war or public danger; nor shall any person be subject for the same offence to be twice put in jeopardy of life or limb; nor shall be compelled in any criminal case to be a witness against himself, nor be deprived of life, liberty, or property, without due process of law; nor shall private property be taken for public use, without just compensation.

__Article the eighth__ ... In all criminal prosecutions, the accused shall enjoy the right to a speedy and public trial, by an impartial jury of the State and district wherein the crime shall have been committed, which district shall have been previously ascertained by law, and to be informed of the nature and cause of the accusation; to be confronted with the witnesses against him; to have compulsory process for obtaining witnesses in his favor, and to have the Assistance of Counsel for his defense.

__Article the ninth__ … In suits at common law, where the value in controversy shall exceed twenty dollars, the right of trial by jury shall be preserved, and no fact tried by a jury, shall be otherwise re-examined in any Court of the United States, then according to the rules of the common law.

__Article the tenth__ ... Excessive bail shall not be required, nor excessive fines imposed, nor cruel and unusual punishments inflicted.

__Article the eleventh__ .... The enumeration in the Constitution, of certain rights, shall not be construed to deny or disparage others retained by the people.

__Article the twelfth__ ... The powers not delegated to the United States by the Constitution, nor prohibited by it to the States, are reserved to the States respectively, or to the people."

ATTEST,

Frederick Augustus Muhlenberg Speaker of the House of Representatives

John Adams, Vice-President of the United States, and President of the Senate.

John Beckley, Clerk of the House of Representatives.
Sam A. Otis, Secretary of the Senate.

One more fact on the Bill of Rights is essential. The "Bill of Rights" is actually the popular name for a joint resolution passed by the first U.S. Congress on September 25, 1789.

The resolution proposed the first set of twelve amendments to the Constitution. Then as now, the process of amending the Constitution required that the resolution be "ratified" or approved by at least three quarters of the states.

Unlike the 10 amendments we know and cherish today as the Bill of Rights, the resolution sent to the states for ratification in 1789, proposed twelve amendments, not just ten. Knowing this ratified body of law consists of just ten amendments, we therefore know that two were not ratified.

When the votes came in, from the 11 states that participated, on December 15, 1791, only the last 10 of the 12 amendments submitted had been ratified. And, so as you scour the original amendments looking for familiar text as in the First Amendment, you will have to cast your eyes to the third amendment proposed to find the contents of the first amendment as ratified.

Thus, the original third amendment, establishing freedom of speech, press, assembly, petition, and the right to a fair and speedy trial became today's First Amendment. Yet, when originally proposed, it was listed as the third amendment.

Chapter 6 The First Ten Restrictions on Central Government Power

The Bill of Rights protects the people

The ten amendments constituting the Bill of Rights are restrictions upon national power. As we see today in America, the elusive notion of the people possessing all power on all issues regarding powers not granted specifically to the Federal Government, falls apart when a president such as the past president simply does not buy that argument. Then, with a corrupt press in his tank, he subtly convinces half of the American people that he is above the law—and that it is perceived by the press and an apparent majority as OK! That, my dear readers, is exactly why some people write books about rights.

The rights and immunities enumerated in the Bill of Rights were already in existence with the ratification of the Constitution but they were not explicit. The people had all their rights and liberties after the war even before they created the Constitution. The Constitution was established to assure these rights, among other purposes, to make the people's liberties secure against oppression by the government, which they were in the process of setting up.

The Bill of Rights was created to make the people more comfortable with the notion that the government would be controlled, by the people, and would operate for the people, and be operated of the people. Let's now take a quick ride through the essence of each of the first ten rights outlined in the Bill of Rights. Americans need every one of these amendments regardless of executive orders to the contrary.

I.
The First Amendment, related to religion, free speech, right of assembly and petition, debars Congress from establishing a religion or

prohibiting free exercise of religion, or abridging the freedom of speech or of the press, or the right of the people peaceably to assemble and to petition the Government for a redress of grievances.

Efforts to check the evil practices of lobbying for most of the 20th century and beyond have been checked when they sought to abridge the right of petition; but freedom of speech and of the press does not permit the publication of libels, blasphemous or other indecent articles, or other publications injurious to morals or private reputation.

A publisher is subject to punishment for contempt if his articles tend to obstruct the administration of justice. The right of free speech does not give immunity for every possible use of language.

II.

The Second Amendment confers upon the people the right to bear arms. It also forbids Congress from infringing upon that right.

III.

The Third Amendment protects the people against military intrusion in their homes. In the colonial period, there were times such as by order of the English quartering act, Americans citizens were forced to make their homes available to British soldiers.

IV.

The Fourth Amendment guarantees the security of the people in their persons, houses, papers, and effects against unreasonable searches and seizures. Almost up to the hour of the evolution the American people from subjugated to free, they had suffered from such injuries at the hands of the British government. The people were determined that their own government should not have power to invade their privacy by "writs of assistance," as general search-warrants were called. John Adams, speaking of James Otis' heroic protest against that practice, declared, "The child *independence* was born on that occasion."

V.

The Fifth Amendment protects the citizen against double jeopardy, self-incrimination, deprivation of life, liberty, or property without due process of law, and loss of property taken for public use. Far-reaching decisions by the courts have protected the citizen under these clauses.

VI.

The Sixth Amendment secures the right of trial by jury, and other rights while under criminal trial. The prohibitions are laid upon Congress, and not upon the States.

VII.

The Seventh Amendment guarantees the rights of citizens in civil trials.

VIII.

The Eighth Amendment prohibits excessive bail and fines, and cruel and unusual punishment. The Supreme Court will interfere with the action of state courts if they impose fines which amount to a deprivation of property without due process of law, but will do this under the Fourteenth Amendment.

IX.

The Ninth Amendment provides that the enumeration of certain rights shall not be construed to deny or disparage other rights retained by the people. "This amendment," said the Supreme Court (Livingston v. Moore, 7 Pet. 551) "indicates that the Federal Constitution is but a delegation of powers, which powers, together with the implied powers, constitute all that the Federal Government has or may presume to exercise." The people retain many rights which are not enumerated, and the Government has no power to interfere with these rights.

X.

The Tenth Amendment is vitally important in preserving the powers of the states and the people against encroachment by Congress [and the president]. It retains to the states or the people all powers not delegated to the United States nor prohibited to the States by the Constitution. In observance of this amendment the Supreme Court has halted attempts to invade the powers of the states, notably in the matter of commerce (there have been numerous examples of this in recent years).

The power of the States to regulate matters of internal police applies not only to the health. morals, and safety of the public, but also to whatever promotes the public peace, comfort, and convenience. State laws enacted under this power may be harsh and oppressive without violating the Constitution, but the restrictions of the Fourteenth Amendment apply.

Chapter 7 The Fourteenth Amendment

Fourteenth amendment assures many rights

Since we have referred to the 14th amendment several times in our discussion of the Bill of Rights, let us cover this amendment out of sequence before we proceed with others.

The 14th Amendment to the U.S. Constitution was ratified on July 9, 1868. Along with the 13th and 15th Amendments, these three are collectively known as the Reconstruction amendments. Why? Their origins were the Civil War Period, and they were all ratified during the post-Civil War era. Although the 14th Amendment was originally intended as a solution to protect the rights of the recently freed slaves, it has continued to play a major role in constitutional politics to this day.

14th Amendment & Civil Rights Act of 1866

Of the three Reconstruction amendments, the 14th is the most complicated and the one that has had the more unforeseen effects. Its broad goal was to reinforce the Civil Rights Act of 1866, which ensured that "all persons born in the United States" were citizens and were to be given "full and equal benefit of all laws."

When the Civil Rights Act landed on Democratic President Andrew Johnson's desk, he vetoed it; Congress, in turn, overrode the veto and the measure became law. Johnson, a Tennessee Democrat, had clashed repeatedly with the Republican-controlled Congress. GOP leaders, fearing Johnson and Southern politicians would attempt to redo the Civil War and undo the first Civil Rights Act, then began work on what would become the 14th Amendment.

Ratification & the states

After passing the Congress in June of 1866, the 14th Amendment went to the states for ratification. As a condition for post-war readmittance to the Union, the former Confederate states were required to approve the amendment.

This idea became a point of contention between Congress and Southern leaders. Connecticut was the first state to ratify the 14th Amendment on June 30, 1866. During the next two years, 28 states would ratify the amendment, though not without incident.

For example, legislatures in Ohio and New Jersey both rescinded their states' pro-amendment votes. In the South, both Louisiana and the Carolinas refused initially to ratify the amendment. Nevertheless, the 14th Amendment was declared formally ratified on July 28, 1868.

Sections of the Amendment

There are four specific sections in the 14th Amendment to the U.S. Constitution. It is generally agreed that the first section is the most important.

Section 1 guarantees citizenship to any and all persons born or naturalized in the U.S. It also guarantees all Americans their constitutional rights and denies states the right to limit those rights through legislation. It also ensures a citizen's "life, liberty, or property" will not be denied without due legal process.

Section 2 states that representation to Congress must be determined based on the whole population. In other words, both white and African American had to be counted equally. Prior to this, African American populations were undercounted when apportioning representation. This section also stipulated that all males 21 years or older were guaranteed the right to vote. Women still had not gained suffrage.

Section 3 was designed to prevent former Confederate officers and politicians from holding office. It states that no one may seek federal elected office if they engaged in rebellion against the U.S.

Section 4 addressed the federal debt accrued during the Civil War. It acknowledged that the federal government would honor its debts. It also stipulated that the government would not honor Confederate debts or reimburse slaveholders for wartime losses.

Section 5 essentially affirms Congress' power to enforce the 14th Amendment through legislation.

There are several key clauses

The four clauses of the first section of the 14th Amendment are the most important because they have repeatedly been cited in major Supreme Court cases concerning civil rights, presidential politics and the right to privacy. Nobody looks at these issues as light matters.

The Citizenship Clause states that "All persons born or naturalized in the United States, and subject to the jurisdiction thereof, are citizens of the United States and of the state wherein they reside." This clause played an important role in two Supreme Court cases: Elk v. Wilkins (1884) addressed citizenship rights of Native Americans, while United States v.
Wong Kim Ark (1898) affirmed citizenship of US-born children of legal immigrants.

The Privileges and Immunities Clause states "No state shall make or enforce any law which shall abridge the privileges or immunities of citizens of the United States." In the Slaughter-House Cases (1873), the Supreme Court recognized a difference between a person's rights as a U.S. citizen and their rights under state law. The ruling held that state laws could not impede a person's federal rights. In McDonald v. Chicago (2010), which overturned a Chicago ban on handguns, Justice Clarence Thomas cited this clause in his opinion supporting the ruling.

The Due Process Clause says no state shall "deprive any person of life, liberty, or property, without due process of law." Although this clause was intended to apply to professional contracts and transactions, over time it has become most closely cited in right-to-privacy cases. Notable Supreme Court cases that have turned on this issue include Griswold v. Connecticut (1965), which overturned a Connecticut ban on the sale of contraception; Roe v. Wade (1973), which overturned a Texas ban on abortion and lifted many restrictions on the practice nationwide; and Obergefell v. Hodges (2015), which held that same-sex marriages deserved federal recognition.

The Equal Protection Clause prevents states from denying "to any person within its jurisdiction the equal protection of the laws." The clause has become most closely associated with civil rights cases, particularly for African Americans. In Plessy v. Ferguson (1898) the Supreme Court ruled that Southern states could enforce racial segregation as long as "separate but equal" facilities existed for blacks and whites.

It wouldn't be until Brown v. Board of Education (1954) that the Supreme Court would revisit this opinion, ultimately ruling that separate facilities were, in fact, unconstitutional. This key ruling opened the door for a number of significant civil rights and affirmative action court cases.

Bush v. Gore (2001) also touched on the equal protection clause when a majority of justices ruled that the partial recount of presidential votes in Florida was unconstitutional because it was not being conducted the same way in all contested locations. The decision essentially decided the 2000 presidential election in George W. Bush's favor.

The Legacy of the 14ᵗʰ Amendment

Over time, numerous lawsuits have arisen that have referenced the 14th Amendment. The fact that the amendment uses the word "state" in the *Privileges and Immunities Clause* -- along with interpretation of the

Due Process Clause -- has meant state power and federal power is subject to the Bill of Rights.

Further, the courts have interpreted the word "person" to include corporations. As a result, corporations are also protected by "due process" along with being granted "equal protection."

While there were other clauses in the amendment, none are as significant as these.

Chapter 8 Amendments After The Bill of Rights

Amendments 11 to 27

The good news for all Americans is that the Constitution implicitly grants rights to the people, who are not necessarily properly served by government. But the idea of explicitly noting the people's basic rights to life, a.k.a. the people's rights and the powers of the people is a great idea. The Bill of Rights provides the needed explicit citation of our rights. Amendments 11 to 27 were not seen as major rights issues when the ten amendments in the Bill of Rights were ratified.

All twenty-seven amendments (Including one to ten – the Bill of Rights) together with the un-amended Constitution equals the Constitution of the US

Let's now take a quick ride through the essence of each of the seventeen amendments ratified one at a time after the Bill of Rights. Each of these rights can be seen as a different release of the Constitution, and in few cases, perhaps a different version. If this were Windows, perhaps it would be version 8 or perhaps version 10.

XI.

The Eleventh Amendment exempts a state from suit by a citizen of another state or a foreigner. It does not deprive the Supreme Court of jurisdiction over suits between states. Nor does it prevent suits against individuals holding official positions under a state, to prevent their committing wrong or trespass under sanction of an unconstitutional statute.

XII.

The Twelfth Amendment was declared in effect September 25, 1804, after a deadlock in the election of a President of the United States. Under the original electoral provision, the elector voted "for two Persons," without designating either for President or Vice President. Jefferson and Burr received an equal number of votes in the election of 1800, and 35 ballots were taken in the House of Representatives before the choice fell to Jefferson. The amendment requires electors to vote separately for President and Vice President.

XIII.

The Thirteenth Amendment abolishes slavery. It differs from the first ten amendments in that it restricts the power of the States as well as that of the national government. It removed legal doubt as to the validity of the Emancipation Proclamation.

The drafting of men for military service does not violate this amendment, since a soldier is not a slave; and the contract of a seaman does not violate the spirit of the amendment.

An act of Congress declaring that no distinction should be made between race or color in denying admission to accommodations and privileges in inns, public conveyances and theaters was held unconstitutional [at this time], because denial of these privileges does not subject any person to any form of servitude or fasten upon him any badge of slavery.

XIV.

The Fourteenth Amendment puts beyond doubt that all persons, white or black, whether former slaves or not, born or naturalized, and owing no allegiance to any foreign power, are citizens of the United States and of the state in which they reside.

The states are prohibited from abridging the immunities of citizens, and from depriving any person of life liberty, or property, without due process of law, or denying to any person equal protection of the laws.

A state law fixing the employment of mine workers at eight hours per day does not contravene the amendment. Statutes regulating the manufacture and sale of goods are within the amendment.

The amendment does not add to constitutional privileges and immunities. The right of suffrage is not one of these rights.

But, soon it would be as the nation was able to address its shortcomings.

XV.

The Fifteenth Amendment provides that the right of citizens to vote shall not be denied or abridged on account of race, color, or previous condition of servitude. It does not confer upon any one the right to vote.

The power to determine qualifications of voters is left to the states; but they may not confine the voting right to white persons.

XVI.

The Sixteenth Amendment is the Income Tax Amendment. It gives Congress the power to tax the incomes of the people and corporations from whatever source derived, without apportionment among the several States. This is not an extension of the taxing power, but it removes all occasion for an apportionment among the states of taxes laid upon incomes. The salaries of United States judges are also taxed but cannot be taxed more than the general public, since Article III of the Constitution provides that they shall not be diminished.

With the sixteenth amendment, Congress and the president were permitted to demand all Americans pay for the government through their incomes.

XVII.

The Seventeenth Amendment changes the mode of election of United States senators. Contests in state legislatures over election of senators had caused great dissatisfaction, and it was believed that election by the people would be an improvement.

Some of us still think it is a good idea for the states to elect Senators. In that way, when a Senator chooses to represent the Senator and not the people, the state, by direction of the people can call back the Senator and appoint one who better represents the people.

From my perspective, this may have originally appeared to be a good amendment but it overall has hurt the people. The people are stuck with a bad senator now for six years. What a shame.

XVIII.

The Eighteenth Amendment provided for prohibition of the manufacture, sale, transportation, importation, and exportation of intoxicating liquors for beverage purposes. Congress and the States were given concurrent power to enforce the amendment. Elliott Ness is the only person who seemed to take the law seriously.

The amendment became effective January 16, 1920. It proved to be unsatisfactory, for many reasons. Confusion arose because of the division of police powers. Enforcement by the national government was impossible. It was urged that this amendment was in conflict with the fifth, by taking property without due process of law. What would be next, outlawing 16-oz soft drinks in NYC?

It conflicted with the provision which makes the acts of Congress the supreme law of the land. Personal liberty, it was claimed, was abridged. On this point the Supreme Court said (Corneli v. Moore, 267 Fed. 456):

"It may be a matter of regret that age-old provisions making for the liberty of action of the citizen have been encroached upon, and to a degree whittled away; but this is not a matter wherein the courts may relieve. It is a political question and not a judicial one."

In other words, the Supreme Court chose not to go along with regular Joe's. They do not always get it right!

After 13 years of trial, with increasing confusion, dissatisfaction, and expense, the Eighteenth Amendment was repealed by the Twenty-first Amendment, which became effective December 5, 1933. Prohibition was gone and Ness, God love him, hopefully retired on a great pension, which unfortunately today could not be afforded by the people.

XIX.

The Nineteenth Amendment provides that the right of United States citizens to vote shall not be denied or abridged by the United States or any state on account of sex. It was declared adopted August 26, 1920. The first proposal to amend the Constitution to provide for woman suffrage was offered by Senator Sargent, of California, in 1878, at the request of Miss Susan B. Anthony.

Fifteen States had granted complete suffrage to women before the amendment was adopted, and in all but nine of the rest they had partial suffrage. A woman was elected to the House of Representatives from Montana in 1916. Women first voted on a national scale in the presidential election of 1920, and apparently their total vote was about 6,000,000. It is believed that at least 12,000,000 women voted in 1932.

When we think of the dumbness that has been so prevalent in our government throughout time, most of the time, it was because of the perception of popular thinking, not because of animus. Blacks were freed by Abraham Lincoln along with a whole lot of white guys who never held anybody, white or black, as a slave.

These white guys were married to white or black women. When color no longer mattered from the laws on the books via amendments, bad residues in old laws were still around and still needed to be fixed. Suffrage was one of them.

Thankfully, black and woman suffrage are now part of the deal. It's been like this for over 100 years so let's get rid of the notion of racism or sexism as precepts of the US government. It has been corrected. Today at worst it is an individual thing.

Just as there are blacks and women who hate whites and men, there surely are whites and men who hate blacks and women. So, what? Should we arrest them all? This amendment is one of those necessary to remove the stigmas of sex and racism in the voting process. America has surely been trying to get itself right.

XX.

The Twentieth Amendment was adopted primarily for the purpose of abolishing "lame duck" sessions of Congress. It changes the dates when the terms of the President, senators and representatives shall begin and end. The presidential term now begins on January 20 every fourth year, and the terms of senators and representatives begin on January 3, the length of term remaining six and two years, respectively. Consequently, a new Congress convenes in the January following the presidential election of the preceding November.

Since only 17 days elapse between the convening of Congress on January 3 and the inauguration of the President on January 20, it is possible that embarrassment may arise in case of delay in counting and declaring the electoral vote, or in electing a President by the House in the event of failure of the electors to elect. The amendment provides that if the President-elect shall have died before inauguration day the Vice President-elect shall be President; and that if a President shall not have been chosen or shall have failed to qualify by inauguration day, the Vice President-elect shall act as President until a President shall have qualified. Congress is authorized to provide for filling a vacancy occurring through failure of both a President-elect and Vice President-elect to qualify, and the person selected shall act until a President or Vice President shall have qualified.

Congress has provided that it shall meet in joint session on January 6 following a presidential election, to count the electoral vote and declare the result. This allows only three days for organization of the House of Representatives by the election of a Speaker. Serious difficulties might arise if the House should fail to organize in time to count the vote, or to elect a President if that duty should fall upon it. Failure of the House to elect a President might be attended by failure of the Senate to elect a Vice President. It is quite conceivable, also, that passions might be aroused if failure to elect a President by a House controlled by one political party should be followed by election of a Vice President by a Senate controlled by another party. It is also conceivable that the two houses of Congress might deadlock upon the selection of a person to fill a vacancy in the Presidency.

XXI.

The Twenty-first Amendment repeals the Eighteenth Amendment which prohibits the transportation or importation into any state of intoxicating liquors in violation of its laws.

XXII

The 22nd amendment limits the president to only two 4-year terms in office. Before the 22nd amendment, Presidents traditionally served two terms, following the example of George Washington. Franklin D Roosevelt broke this tradition during his presidency and served four terms, as World War II and the Great Depression convinced him to run for a third and fourth term, since the country was in crisis. After FDR died in 1945, many Americans began to recognize that having a president serve more than eight years was bad for the country. This led to the 22nd amendment, which was passed by Congress in 1947 and ratified by the states by 1951

XXIII

The 23rd Amendment to the US Constitution was passed by Congress on March 29, 1961. It provides the District of Columbia with the ability to vote for president and vice-president. Up until this time, individuals who lived in the District of Columbia were unable to vote for the president since they did not live in a state. Presidential electors were determined based on the number of representatives and senators associated with a particular state. This set the number of electors for the District of Columbia equal to that of the least populous state, which means that it has three electors.

XXIV

The 24th amendment was important to the Civil Rights Movement as it ended mandatory poll taxes that prevented many African Americans from voting. The rationale for the amendment was that poll taxes, combined with grandfather clauses and intimidation, effectively prevented African Americans from having any sort of political power, especially in the South. When the 24th amendment passed, five southern states, Virginia, Alabama, Texas, Arkansas, and Mississippi still had poll taxes. Most Southern states, at one time or another had poll taxes and in severe cases, had cumulative poll taxes that required the voter to pay taxes not just from that year, but also previous years they had not voted.

Admittedly poll taxes are inherently unfair but Americans being lied to by government is also unfair, and unfortunately, there are American parties that try to trick the least capable of US to discern the message that they will lose their ability to live if X is not elected over Y, even if X is a rapist, a murderer, or a simple political cheat—a thief so to speak.

All men are created equal for sure, and poll taxes may not be proper but permitting the simple minded among us to vote for such important notions is also not fair as they are affected by the messages of the tricksters.

Today, we should have a means of telling a lie from the truth, and any politician who lies should be disqualified from the opportunity of office. If it is discerned by judges that such messages would cause those who would otherwise not know better that they had been lied to then, and I do not know how to do this, their votes would not count. We the People want an informed electorate to vote for important offices. We should figure out how to eliminate those who have no clue who is running from being the deciding voters.

That is the truth. Unfortunately, our laws do not force politicians to tell the truth or go to jail. Either we have huge prison penalties for lying officials in office and in their candidacies or we need poll gimmicks to prevent the easily influenced by lies to not influence important elections. You tell me how we do that? Otherwise, the least capable people in America may choose who runs our country!

XXV

If the President of the United State dies in office, the Vice President will assume the position of the presidency. Although this is the law today, this was not always the case prior to the 25th amendment. In fact, it was never actually clear in the Constitution that the Vice-President takes over for the President.

The Vice-President has taken over for the President several times in our history, usually after the president has been killed or dies of sickness and the first time this happened was when John Tyler, the 10th president, became president after William Henry Harrison died after a month as President. The 25th amendment allows for the Vice President to become president in the event of death, resignation, removal from office or impairment that prevents the current president from fulfilling his or her duties.

The Vice-presidency had been clearly defined by the 12th amendment as the running mate of the sitting president. As such, there is no risk that a member of the opposing party will gain the presidency in the event of the president being unable to serve his or her duties. Among the more important provisions of the 25th amendment are the provisions for the "Acting President."

During this condition, the Vice-President temporarily assumes the role of the President as it is assumed that the President is unable to fulfill his or her duties at the moment but will be able to in the very near future.

The 25th amendment was adopted by the states in 1967 with Nebraska and Wisconsin being the first states to ratify it and Nevada the 38th and last state needed to have a ¾ majority

XXVI

The 26th Amendment to the US Constitution was passed by Congress on March 23, 1971 and ratified on July 1, 1971, all during the Vietnam War. The amendment provided the right to vote to individuals who were eighteen years of age. Previous to this, the 14th Amendment had set the voting age at 21. Very strong feelings existed that if people were old enough to serve and die for their country, they should also be able to vote for those people sending them to war.

XXVII

The 27th Amendment to the US Constitution prohibits any law that increases or decreases the salary of members of Congress from taking effect until the start of the next set of terms of office for Representatives. It is the most recent amendment to the United States Constitution.

It was submitted by Congress to the states for ratification on September 25, 1789, and became part of the United States Constitution in May 1992, a record-setting period of 202 years, 7 months and 12 days.

As we examine rights in this book, the politicians of yesteryear submitted this item to be in the original bill of rights as the second amendment. It was rejected then and somewhat recently has passed and thus its new sequence is amendment # 27.

Conclusion

The conclusion for this chapter is mostly written by Sol Bloom. It is from his 150th Anniversary Book re-mastered by Lets Go Publish! And titled, *Sol Bloom's … Epoch Story of the Constitution.*

From the time that I read his book I have been impressed with the late Congressman Bloom. He is in my opinion a 1937 version of America's founders. I have used many of his thoughts in the chapters we have already discussed. I give you many of his original thoughts in the conclusion below, though I have altered some of the notions as written to fit the times. To get the original, feel free to read Bloom's book.

https://www.amazon.com/Sol-Blooms-Epoch-Story-Constitution/dp/0989995763

Here is the Chapter Conclusion, which not so coincidentally is also the conclusion of Sol Bloom's Book on the Constitution.

"As the symmetry of arrangement and beautiful co-ordination of motion in the several governments constituting the American system may be compared with the solar system.

"As the Sun is the center of attraction and controlling power that binds and moves the planets in one system, so the People are the center and controlling power that binds and moves their governments in one system.

"The Law which the solar system obeys is not written, but its operation is partly disclosed and partly understood. The Law which the American political system obeys is partly written, for all men to read. It is the Constitution of the United States.

"The limits of the powers of the Sun and the People are not known. They have never been tested to the limit. The composition of the Sun is hidden in Nature. The composition of the People is hidden in human nature.

"Reason assumes that the Sun has powers beyond those known to us. Reason reinforced by knowledge asserts that the People have reserved powers which never have been expressed in written law.

"The United States and the States may be compared to planets revolving around their Sun, the People.

"In order to comprehend the peculiar nature of the American system it must be borne in mind that the States existed before the United States was created. It was to bind them together, to swing them into their coordinated orbits that the Union was perfected.

"Some of the powers possessed by the People are exerted in the States. Others are kept in reserve.

"The powers necessary to bind the States together in one solar Union are set forth in the Constitution. All other powers are kept in reserve.

"The States perform certain functions which the United States cannot perform. The United States performs functions which the States separately cannot perform. The People retain a sphere of personal liberties into which neither the States nor the United States can enter.

"The law which controls the solar system is divine, and therefore perfect. The law which controls the American political system is human, and therefore imperfect. But under a trial of 150 years [when Bloom wrote his book in 1937], it has been found to approach more nearly the symmetry of the law that rules the universe than any other emanation of the human mind and will.

"Several unique features of the Constitution distinguish it from any previous inventions in the art of government. Among these are: The Constitution binds individuals as well as States. Under it all individuals have equal duties and rights.

"The legislative, executive, and judicial powers are lodged in separate bodies of public servants whose powers and duties compel them to check and balance one another. No uncontrolled power is lodged in any one. The written Constitution is made paramount to any legislative, executive, or judicial authority.

"A court is created with power to hold all authorities within their allotted spheres, and this court itself is bound to remain within its allotted sphere. The Constitution contains within itself a method whereby it may be amended by the People.

"These principles, never practiced before, are the bone and sinew of a fabric suitable to a nation whose government obeys those whom it rules, and whose people rule the government which they obey."

End of Sol Bloom's Conclusion.

Don't we all wish that we could write as well as Sol Bloom. He has helped us all understand why being an American, born of the founders and of Sol Bloom's sweat labor, is such a big deal. We Americans are all so lucky!

Chapter 9 Summary of All Proposed Constitutional Amendments

Can such great works be summarized?

Without reading the full text of an amendment, one cannot gain its full impact on the freedoms and rights of American citizens. Even then, for average Joe's, such verbiage is tough to read.

Though the amendments to the Constitution can be summarized, it would be for purposes other than understanding their full impact on the nation. It would be for a perspective on what they contain from cover to cover without having to read all between.

Like all summaries, citizens get to read about the nature and the planned purposes of the amendments even without reading them. So, summaries do have value.

The summaries do not give the notion of the full text of the principles of our government for sure but they show where correction was needed and applied. The founders admitted that they were imperfect. All humans are imperfect. So, when the founders created the Articles of Confederation to govern the United States, it was round one of an effort to make a more perfect democratic republic.

As humans, after a time, even the founders doubted the perfection of their resulting work. No human delivers perfection ever—only God. So, should the founders have given up and said c'est la vie (French for that's just how it is)—when the Articles of Confederation were deemed imperfect? Should they have gone home, opened up a bottle of the finest wine and approved of themselves to the bottom of the bottle. Or should they have taken another try to do better? Of course, we all vote for the latter and so did the founders.

There is nothing like the original and that is why in the preceding chapters we discuss the Constitution as written, prior to the Bill of Rights. The Bill of Rights certainly has helped the hoi polloi and the hoity-toity understand this major historical document far better.

On the Internet in the fine documents of our founding, there is much text which further explains the position of the Bill of Rights in context with the US Constitution. The Constitution improved on the Articles of Confederation, and the Bill of Rights clarified for the common man, a number of key rights inherent in the Constitution.

The Bill of Rights has been fully explained in their purpose and their meaning in this and preceding chapters of this book. It is a feel-good document for scholars but it is an essential document for Americans searching for just a few well written sentences describing their rights.

The Bill of Rights changed the Constitution to make it clear that Americans had specific rights, not just those denied to the federal government through the Constitution. The US government, over the next two hundred plus years from the Constitution's ratification found just seventeen additional changes to the Constitution necessary once the Bill of Rights became the first ten amendments.

These of course were in addition to the ten amendments (changes) already included in the Bill of Rights. These twenty-seven amendments make the US Constitution an even better, and an even more perfect union of the United States of America than the Constitution alone, when it replaced the Articles of Confederation.

Let's take another quick snapshot of the entire twenty-seven Amendments including the first ten, the Bill of Rights. Besides the Constitution itself, these are the outward principles upon which our freedoms and our liberties are cast.

The Bill of Rights in summary:

— **Amendment I:** Freedom of speech, religion, press, petition, assembly.
— **Amendment II:** Right to bear arms and militia.

— **Amendment III**: Quartering of soldiers.
— **Amendment IV:** Warrants and searches.
— **Amendment V:** Individual debt and double jeopardy.
— **Amendment VI:** Speedy trial, witnesses and accusations.
— **Amendment VII:** Right for a jury trial.
— **Amendment VIII:** Bail and fines.
— **Amendment IX**: Existence of other rights for the people
— **Amendment X:** Power reserved to the states and people.

Later amendments in summary

— **Amendment XI:** Suits against states.
— **Amendment XII:** Election of executive branch.
— **Amendment XIII:** Prohibition of slavery.
— **Amendment XIV:** Privileges or immunities, due process, elections and debt: Consists of 5 sections and defines: (1) Citizenship (2) Apportionment of representatives among the states, (3) Rules for being a senator or representative, (4) Validity of the public debt, (5) Congressional enforcement of this Article.
— **Amendment XV:** Race and the right to vote.
— **Amendment XVI:** US Income tax enabled.
— **Amendment XVII:** Senator election change and number.
— **Amendment XVIII:** Prohibition on sale of alcohol
— **Amendment XIX:** Gender and the right to vote.
— **Amendment XX:** "Lame duck" Congress eliminated.
— **Amendment XXI:** Repeal of Amendment XVIII (Prohibition).
— **Amendment XXII:** Limit of Presidential terms.
— **Amendment XXIII:** Election rules for the District of Columbia
— **Amendment XXIV:** Taxes and the right to vote.
— **Amendment XXV:** Rules of Presidential succession.
— **Amendment XXVI:** Age and the right to vote.
— **Amendment XXVII:** Pay raises and Congress

Amendments Never Ratified

Besides the above summary of the constitutional body of law, six other amendments have been proposed to the Constitution that have not been ratified and thus do not represent the law of the land. The entire text of these amendments is included in Appendix G.

The original first amendment was never ratified. It set the ratio of representatives of Congress to constituents. If this amendment had made it to the bill of Rights, and been ratified, the number of members of the House of Representatives could by now be over 6,000, compared to the present 435. As apportioned by the 2000 Census, each member of the House currently represents about 650,000 people.

The original second amendment passed by Congress which was not ratified, was eventually ratified as the 27th amendment of the United States 203 years after it was first offered. It has to do with Congressional Salaries.

What does all this mean?

We have examined the founding and the revolution and the articles and precepts in the Constitution as the primary law of the land. We have also examined the Bill of rights in detail and the other amendments to the Constitution in summary form.

For you, as you have read this material, you are a member of a more informed electorate. When you get the government you deserve, because you care about America and you are learning more and more about your country, when you get the government you deserve, it can be a much better government.

Chapter 10 Constitutional Rights, Powers and Duties

The people or the government?

The Bill of Rights is the collective name for the first ten amendments to the United States Constitution. It helps to repeat that often when one is learning the concepts of our founding government. As you may know from earlier reading in this book, the Bill of Rights was proposed to quiet the fears of Anti-Federalists who had opposed Constitutional ratification.

The ten (originally twelve) amendments were brought forth to guarantee a number of personal freedoms (rights), limit the government's power in judicial and other proceedings, and reserve some powers to the states and the public.

Originally the amendments applied only to the federal government. However, most were subsequently applied to the government of each state by way of the Fourteenth Amendment to the Constitution, through a process known as incorporation.

Let's recap how these rights were introduced to Congress. On June 8, 1789, Representative James Madison introduced a series of thirty-nine amendments (Lots more than the twelve which were approved) to the constitution in the House of Representatives. Among his recommendations Madison proposed opening up the Constitution and inserting specific rights directly into the articles of the Constitution. His notions limited the power of Congress beginning in Article One, Section 9. At the time, the founders figured Congress had the real power and there would be no need to limit the power of the chief executive as Congress could theoretically do that by itself.

Seven of these limitations would eventually become part of the ten ratified Bill of Rights as amendments. Ultimately, on September 25,

1789, Congress approved twelve articles of amendment to the Constitution and submitted them to the states for ratification. Many of the Anti-Federalists wanted the Constitution itself, within in its main body, not in adjunct form, to delineate the rights of the people of the nation. Madison's original proposal had provided for that.

Contrary to Madison's original proposal that the articles be incorporated into the main body of the Constitution, they were eventually proposed as "supplemental" additions to it. On December 15, 1791, Articles Three–Twelve, having been ratified by the required number of states, became renumbered as Amendments One–Ten of the Constitution. These ten ratified amendments were the Bill of Rights as passed and became a part of the Constitution forever.

On May 7, 1992, after an unprecedented period of 202 years, 225 days, the original submitted and not ratified Amendment # 2, known then as Article Two crossed the Constitutional threshold for ratification and became the Twenty-Seventh Amendment and the last amendment as of 2014. As a result, the original Article One (the original 1st amendment) alone remains unratified and still pending before the states.

The Bill of Rights enumerates freedoms not explicitly indicated in the main body of the Constitution, such as freedom of religion, freedom of speech, a free press, and free assembly; the right to keep and bear arms; freedom from unreasonable search and seizure, security in personal effects, and freedom from warrants issued without probable cause; indictment by a grand jury for any capital or "infamous crime"; guarantee of a speedy, public trial with an impartial jury; and prohibition of double jeopardy.

The rights of the people

In addition, the Bill of Rights reserves for the people any rights not specifically mentioned in the Constitution and reserves all powers not specifically granted to the federal government for the people or the States. The Bill was influenced by George Mason's 1776 Virginia Declaration of Rights, the English Bill of Rights 1689, and earlier English political documents such as Magna Charta (1215 A.D.).

The Bill of Rights had little judicial impact for the first 150 years of its existence, but was the basis for many Supreme Court decisions of the 20th and 21st centuries. One of the first fourteen copies of the Bill of Rights is on public display at the National Archives in Washington, D.C.

What specific rights / powers do we the people have and what rights / powers do we the people not have? What rights / powers does the government have and which ones does it not have? All Americans should want to know the answers to those questions.

And so, we have a ton of rights and powers to discuss in the remainder of this chapter. Since this is a book about the Bill of Rights it is a good idea to define a right as well as a power or a duty so that we get a clear picture of what the Constitution and the Bill of Rights delivers to us

What is a right? A right is a moral or legal entitlement to have or obtain something or to act in a certain way

What is a power? A power is the ability to do something or act in a particular way, especially as a faculty or quality. Also, a power can be defined as the possession of control or command over others; authority.

What is a duty? A duty is a moral or legal obligation; a responsibility. It can also be a task or action that someone is required to perform.

The following outline describes in brief the more important rights, powers, and duties recognized or established in the U.S. Constitution, in Common Law as it existed at the time the U.S. Constitution was adopted, or as implied therein.

Not included in this outline are certain "internal" or administrative rights and powers that pertain to the various elements of government within each level with respect to each other. This chapter is just big enough to give us a proper perspective on what the Constitution along with the Bill of Rights provide for all Americans.

Chapter 11 Bill of Rights Makes the Constitution OK for All!

The fight over the Bill of Rights

Now, that you and I have exhaustingly traversed multiple chapters, in search of the perfect founding of our nation along with a "perfect" Bill of Rights, should we believe that we have found it? I say yes!

The Constitution of the United States of America contains the Bill of Rights. Not only does it contain the whole Bill of Rights but it is based on a long line of other historical documents that add even more meaning to the Constitution and American rights as we find ourselves at times trying to understand exactly what the founders meant here and there. And, thus it has been quite proper to discuss most of these documents before we move to the real purpose of this book, The US Bill of Rights.

The "perfect Bill of Rights," is thus based on the "perfect Constitution." In its own rules, the Constitution prescribes a way for it to be changed, as long as the people agree. Who can ask for anything more?

In order for the Constitution to have been ratified and to become the operating supreme law of the Land of the USA, the founders convinced detractors that they would use the rules in the Constitution itself to change it to suit the detractor's needs. The Bill of Rights in fact, was the first set of changes to the US Constitution, and it satisfied the objections of the original detractors. If the founders had not done some good convincing, the Constitution would exist only in the history books and not as the law of the land.

The Constitution offers no opportunity for the congress or the president to choose to act other than directed by the articles within this document as well as the laws enacted by the Congress. In terms of the forty-fourth President, we know that there are a number of accusations of lawlessness. Nobody other than the people can change the Constitution—even the president of the United States, as hard as he may try.

The laws broken by the prior administration include violations of the pure Constitution and a number of other laws that have been enacted by Congress, which the past president, as all presidents has taken an oath to enforce. The past president had no problem with calling a weak Congress's bluff and so he chose his laws carefully, and thus, he reigned, un-impeached.

However, more and more citizens have found that the lawlessness of the Executive Branch was a little too much to stomach. In the America if which the people have understood for years, they did not have a need to demanding Congress act to assure that the Constitution in totality is upheld and not disregarded as trivial by the president. The election of Donald J. Trump over Hillary R. Clinton for some in Congress was the first time that they got to fully understand the frustrations of the American people with a lawless administration.

The Constitution, though a phenomenally "more perfect" instrument of government for America than the Articles of Confederation, is still not 100% perfect. Nothing is perfect! As I like to say in its defense, it is more perfect than any other supreme body of law in any other country, including Bimini, which is a beautiful island in the Bahamas—where I think I would rather be than right here, right now!

If this were not so, I too would definitely be seeking refuge in Bimini, or the next most free country in the world. Right now, because of our Constitution, and the expressed Bill of Rights, we would find the only country that provides full freedom and liberty in all cases to be the United States of America. Though some politicians may have bought the stamp, there is no expiration date on the United States.

Americans paying attention know that the best set of laws for both the hoi polloi (regular people) and the hoity-toity (the elite among us) is our one of a kind US Constitution including its Bill of Rights and subsequent amendments.

The Bill of Rights is essential in that it spells out in bold detail, the fundamental rights of all Americans including the rights of free assembly, free speech, freedom to practice religion, and many other rights including the right to bear arms. Some presidents of recent time would like to do away with these rights.

Many ask why, with such a fine Constitution is a separate *"Bill of Rights"* required? If the Constitution is almost perfect, why was it not enough? Why is it not enough? "Why did we ever need a *Bill of Rights*? We have broached this subject in past chapters but let's take it head on again.

In this modern era, where all traditional values are questioned, there is a film and a video game known as the *Bill of Rights*. Perhaps you know of this. Perhaps you have seen it or heard about it. Both media notions (film & video game) attempt to tell the story about a struggle among the founders and the framers of the US Constitution that nearly tore the nation apart. We have discussed this but let's go again.

It was even before the US had a Constitution to assure its future. Toward the end of the 16-minute documentary, the *Bill of Rights* is described as "absolutely essential to our national character."

When the founders were founding the nation, there was no notion of political parties, and that is why the brave men of those times were able to come together to delineate a set of laws that would be able to guide America forever. There were no Republicans and there were no Democrats. There was no partisan politics because there were no partisans. The founders built it that way. Everybody was for America.

Even then, of course there was the risk of a scoundrel in an important office, who might be un-American, and that scoundrel, even if he were the president, himself, might choose to ignore the laws of the country, passed or not passed in his or her administration.

Therefore, the folks at that time, some who believed the Constitution was perfect, and others who thought that our rights needed to be declared outwardly in a positive sense, needed to come together.

The Constitution gave the people all the power but to be fair, specific important rights which many call freedoms and liberties, were not delineated. And, so an errant judge in the future, wrong as he or she might be, could decree that there is no right in the Constitution guaranteeing your freedom of speech or assembly. The judge would be wrong but, then what happens when you find yourself in prison? What do you have to say you have the right?

The Bill of Rights therefore specifically, forcefully, and more authoritatively defines the fundamental rights of the American people. Some people in 1787 had a major issue about whether the US Constitution restricted government powers sufficiently enough to assure that Americans had perpetual liberty under the law. Today's citizens can understand why!

If Government had no power to restrict the power of the people, then why should the people need a specific bill of rights? The simple answer is that after hundreds of years of tyranny in their home countries, the colonists trusted nobody, and they therefore recognized the possibility of an errant judge or powerful government of the future misunderstanding the Constitution, and going it alone without the Congress or the people.

The framers of The Constitution gave no implicit rights to government other than those so enumerated specifically in the Constitution. There were few of these as enumerated in prior chapters. So, many of the framers did not believe that the people needed a bill of rights since government could theoretically never take away the inalienable rights the people already possessed.

The Constitution gave the government no power to override the will of the people. Others were concerned that since people are people, scoundrels might emerge as leaders and the people would have no backup column to present to prove their rights. And, so many smart Americans looked for a specific Bill of Rights! I think we are better off with it than we would be without it.

Implication or Specification?

The battle of whether a Bill of Rights was necessary during the founding and framing of the Constitution is a matter of implication or specification. Those who believed the government was sufficiently verboten from taking away individual liberty saw no reason to specify (specification) the liberties that could not be taken away.

Their answer was "no liberties" can be taken from the people since the Constitution in raw form, un-amended, implicitly defers rights not given to the government as rights which the people implicitly possess. Yet, implicit or explicit, when quoted, we all like to have an explicit quote upon which to base our contention.

Well, the explicits and the implicits got their day of discussion and our founders worked it out for the good of all to come up with something that would work. Out of their compromise (The Great Compromise) came one of our nation's most central documents and the foundation for some of our most celebrated freedoms. The document produced to represent their thoughts is forever known as the *Bill of Rights.*

Whether it was needed logically or not needed logically, it is the Bill of Rights nonetheless. It guaranteed the ratification of The Constitution. It was enough to convince the patriots that the Constitution was perfect enough to be approved.

They felt the base Constitution was not enough

Americans wanted written assurances that the rights they fought for as colonists against Britain in the American Revolution would never be taken away. They believed their rights should be protected by a written document. The Bill of Rights plus the Constitution serve that purpose. Add the additional 17 amendments and you've got a winning trifecta.

Without and explicit bill that listed the rights of the people, some of the states had refused to ratify the Constitution. They did not like that in its first cut, a national Bill of Rights was not included. Thus, the Bill of Rights was deemed to be an essential ingredient to having a Constitution pass the states for ratification.

Without the *Bill of Rights,* we would have never been able to ratify the Constitution and thus we would never have been able to add the necessary stability to our nation to fend of all foes and grow more and more powerful. The Constitution and the specifics in the *Bill of Rights* and the other seventeen amendments have helped our country survive during the times of instability, confusion, and partial insanity concerning how to properly organize and run the nation.

The *Bill of Rights* was carved out after the Constitution had been written. And, though it is deemed by many to be an integral "part" of the Constitution, when offered to the people, it was created independently of the Constitution and presented as an add-on, though a very necessary add-on.

The *Bill of Rights* indeed consists of the first ten approved / ratified amendments to the US Constitution. The original framers trusted that we would never turn on the precepts in the Constitution. Those insisting on the need for a Bill of Rights wanted to assure themselves that we could not even find a minor loophole in the Constitution to limit our rights.

We all know, and quite often in this book, we have demonstrated, how the Constitution guarantees every American certain basic rights, including: freedom of speech, freedom of religion, the right to assembly, the right to a jury trial, etc. These and many other rights are implicitly protected by our Constitution. But these freedoms, though implicit, were not explicitly stated in the original version of the Constitution. It took the *Bill of Rights* to mention them explicitly.

You may have already read the full Constitution. If so, you know that nothing was written in the Constitution to implicitly or specifically grant the freedoms in the Bill of Rights to all Americans. In fact, as noted, many of the Framers of the Constitution were dead set against including such a bill in the document even if provided as amendments. Like the old TV ad once said, the framers would answer: "It's in there!"

The framers were very smart people. They knew that when they had written the Constitution, they had implicitly granted all those provisions in the Bill of Rights simply by denying government such rights. In truth, implicit provisions are far more powerful and long-serving than those explicitly provided. But, with anything implicit, the government must be even more honest. With "explicit," government would have no choice.

Honest regular people at that time, and even in this time, looking for truth have a tough time understanding and trusting implicit notions. And, so the explicit provisions of the Bill of Rights helped many Americans, who did not profess to be Constitutional scholars to lean towards the ratification of the Constitution when ten important rights of the people were explicitly noted.

Thus, as the debate ensued, the non-trusting were compelled by their very nature to demand as many explicit provisions from the new government as possible. The colonists did not trust any government at the time—even if their favorite neighbor were president.

As we all know, humans have limited attention spans. Worse than that, historical governments have most often gone bad over time. So, why would the regular folks in America back those wanting votes for the Constitution without "proper" guarantees for liberty and freedom over time?

And, so a look back does say that a Bill of Rights needed to be created and added to the Constitution. James Madison, one of the major authors of the Federalist Papers, and a great patriot, who eventually became the fourth President of the United States, was enlisted to write many of the precepts in the Bill of Rights. Like Alexander Hamilton, he was a phenomenal writer. He is credited with being the primary author of the Constitution and so he is known by historians as the "Father of the Constitution."

Ironically, Madison, in his personal thoughts, did not think a Bill of Rights was necessary. He took issue, though lightly, with those who felt that the Constitution needed to grant rights. Instead, he felt that the people had all the rights, according to the Constitution and the government had no rights other than those explicitly granted by the people. Yet, Madison was also a reasonable man.

Madison would have been against any Bill of Rights and the document that emerged from the Constitutional Convention in 1787 (The Constitution) reflected his full conviction. He believed the Constitution as it was written already spelled out what the Federal Government could do and could not do. He believed that if it wasn't in that document, it wasn't any of the Federal Government's business. No further protection was necessary. He was right logically, but as noted *implicit* was not a convincing argument for the people. I thank the Lord that Madison changed his mind.

Madison would have been fervently in favor of a Bill of Rights if he lived in the 19th, 20th, or 21st century. James Madison never met a 20th or 21st Century leftist politician looking for an excuse to break through the limitations on government provided in the Constitution to further the cause of communism.

These scoundrels love their rights yet want the rights of others taken away to suit their selfish interests. Some, even today, believe that the Bill of Rights has only postponed the villains, who sometimes even outwardly shows disdain for the freedoms granted to Americans by the Constitution.

As recently as late May 2014, for example, the past president, who claims even today to be a constitutional scholar, challenged the notion of Article II of the Constitution regarding two Senators from each state. The President said it is unfair that hugely populated Democratic States such as New York and California get just two Senators when they have lots more people. If you are reading this book in 2017, it would save some research for you to know that the past president, who no longer presides as I am writing this book, is a leftist long before he is a happy American.

There was concern by me and others that this President, with a lack of any deep love for America and the Constitution, try by Executive Order to change the Constitution? We are very pleased that he ran out of time.

The President had already done this with other laws such as those pertaining to immigration and social issues. This, of course is why his administration was considered lawless. It helps to remember that many colonists were concerned that a strong national government was a threat to individual rights and that a president might attempt to become a king, and that strengthened their demand for more explicit rights. Pre-Obama this was not ever an issue in America.

Thankfully no American President so far at least, has ever tried to convince the people he or she should be King or Queen of America. The people were concerned that if this past president's surrogate became president then we might one day soon have a queen. Her name would not be Diana or Camilla but it might be Hillary. Somebody came by and trumped her efforts to be Queen of America!

Because of things we have seen and inactions we have suffered from a wimpy do-nothing Congress, the implicit v explicit dialogue results are in. To most conservative Americans, it is far better to explicitly state rights than to have a politician motivated by political opportunism take matters into their own hands.

Why is it that the courts, using impartiality and "superior" judgment today always break decisions on party lines? Why is it that America and Americans are not the primary focus of the legislature and the courts?

Well, this is not the right book to fully discuss this particular matter, but if I had my way, I would fire the press first. They are so corrupt that they stink like dead fish. Congress is only a short whiff away from being as bad. Would it not be wonderful if political party affiliation and agendas were not how the courts or the Senate or the House would decide issues that are substantive to citizens?

The leaders and the people in colonial time had integrity as a real virtue. Their moms and dads helped them gain such virtue. Even those not on your side were good people and good enough to work for compromises that helped all Americans—not just the Democratic Party.

George Mason, a Virginia delegate vigorously disagreed with James Madison on the notion of a Bill of Rights, yet both were honorable in their disagreement. Mason was not so sure that the new government would provide anything better than the rights the British had provided, and then took back when it was convenient. Madison knew the inherent logic in the Constitution should work for all Americans.

Despite being wounded in spirit and in their wallets, Americans in the eighteenth century all knew that a long and bloody war to win independence had only recently ended. Though Madison et al believed that they had protected Americans with the magical text of The Constitution, Mason and others wanted to explicitly ensure that the new government could not erase the freedoms the patriots had fought so hard to secure.

George Mason declared that he would rather "chop off my right hand" than support a Constitution that did not include a Bill of Rights. What a great patriot!

If we are looking for forefathers of things like Articles and Declarations and Constitutions, we might well credit George Mason as the *Father of the Bill of Rights,* regardless of how active his pen was in the process.

Depending on your level of trust in the positive precepts of the Constitution as originally written, it is reasonable to believe that the more assurances of freedom the better. Those patriots looking for more assurances won and the major product of their work, The Bill of Rights was added to the Constitution as the first ten amendments on December 15, 1791.

The fact that the Constitution did not include a Bill of Rights to specifically protect Americans' hard-won rights had certainly sparked the most heated debates during the ratification process. Now that we know there is such a Bill; what rights do they give?

Let's go over a few for a second or third time as all of us have a tendency to forget important things until we realize how important they really are.

Rights from the Bill of Rights

As previously noted, the Bill of Rights are the first ten amendments (changes) to the United States Constitution. Madison saw no real problem with the Bill of Rights other than redundancy; for he already believed they existed implicitly within the Constitution.

Rather than risk destroying the Constitution, Jefferson, out of town during the debate about the Bill of Rights, wrote to Madison advocating their inclusion: "Half a loaf is better than no bread. If we cannot secure all our rights, let us secure what we can." So, Madison introduced the Bill of Rights as a series of amendments on June 8, 1789 in the First Federal Congress.

Who wrote the Bill of Rights? George Mason, who would not sign the Constitution without the Bill of Rights and James Madison, who felt they were not needed, are considered by historians to be among the two primary authors of the twelve articles in the original Bill of Rights.

Ten of the amendments of the twelve were ratified without much debate and they became the Bill of Rights in 1791. These amendments specify rights of citizens explicitly by their content and implicitly by "further" limiting the powers of the federal government. They protect the rights of all citizens, residents and visitors on United States territory. More people today understand the Bill of Rights even more than those that understand the full impact of the US Constitution.

About the Bill of Rights?

So, what is meant by the term Bill of Rights? It represents the full notion of the first ten amendments to the United States Constitution. Amendments are supposed to be changes even though Madison believed these ten Amendments, and the rights they gave American citizens existed implicitly in the original drafting of the US Constitution. Madison saw the Bill as being redundant; but redundancy on a topic such as liberty and freedom was OK with him. In the end, James Madison was OK with the Bill of Rights.

These amendments, known as the Bill of Rights were specific rights to be granted to citizens even if they had not conceived that they already had the rights simply because the Constitution granted no such rights to government.

The Bill of Rights in summary, even today, explicitly limits the federal government's powers. It protects the rights of the people by preventing Congress from abridging freedom of speech, freedom of the press, freedom of assembly, freedom of religious worship, and the right to bear arms, and many other rights as noted in the ten very specific amendments.

For example, the Bill of Rights prevents unreasonable search and seizure, cruel and unusual punishment, and self-incrimination, and it guarantees due process of law and a speedy public trial with an impartial jury. Implicitly the Constitution itself gave the people these rights but for the people, having the issue presented and the right demonstrated meant a lot more than wondering what was what.

In addition, the Bill of Rights states that "the enumeration in the Constitution, of certain rights, shall not be construed to deny or disparage others (rights) retained by the people," and reserves all powers not specifically granted to the Federal government to the citizenry or States.

The original Ten Amendments to the Constitution, The Bill of Rights was introduced by Madison and passed by Congress September 25, 1789. These amendments came into effect when three/fourths of the states ratified them on December 15, 1791—four years after the Constitution had been created.

LETS GO PUBLISH! Books by Brian Kelly
(Sold at www.bookhawkers.com; Amazon.com, and Kindle.).